The **COLLEGE** SOLUTION

Second Edition

The **COLLEGE** SOLUTION

A Guide for Everyone Looking for the Right School at the Right Price

Second Edition

Lynn O'Shaughnessy

Vice President, Publisher: Tim Moore
Associate Publisher and Director of Marketing: Amy Neidlinger
Executive Editor: Jim Boyd
Editorial Assistant: Pamela Boland
Operations Manager: Jodi Kemper
Assistant Marketing Manager: Megan Graue
Cover Designer: Chuti Prasertsith
Managing Editor: Kristy Hart
Project Editor: Andy Beaster
Copy Editor: Geneil Breeze
Proofreader: Sarah Kearns
Senior Indexer: Cheryl Lenser
Compositor: Nonie Ratcliff
Manufacturing Buyer: Dan Uhrig

ISBN-10: 0-13-294467-7
ISBN-13: 978-0-13-294467-0

Pearson Education LTD.
Pearson Education Australia PTY, Limited.
Pearson Education Singapore, Pte. Ltd.
Pearson Education Asia, Ltd.
Pearson Education Canada, Ltd.
Pearson Educatión de Mexico, S.A. de C.V.
Pearson Education—Japan
Pearson Education Malaysia, Pte. Ltd.

Library of Congress Cataloging-in-Publication Data

O'Shaughnessy, Lynn, 1955-
  The college solution : a guide for everyone looking for the right school at the right price / Lynn O'Shaughnessy. -- 2nd ed.
    p. cm.
  ISBN 978-0-13-294467-0 (pbk. : alk. paper)
  1. College student orientation--United States. 2. College choice--United States. 3. Student aid--United States. I. Title.
  LB2343.32.O82 2012
  378.73--dc23
                              2012002780

To Caitlin, Ben, and Bruce

*And to my parents, Jacquelin and
Vincent P. O'Shaughnessy*

Contents

Acknowledgments

When my parents contemplated sending their five children to college, they concluded that my mother would have to start teaching again to help pay the education bills. My parents had always been frugal—growing up in St. Louis I don't recall ever eating steak—but frugality couldn't cover what they faced: 20 years' worth of college costs.

My mother, who had left the teaching profession when her oldest child (that's me) was born, headed back to the classroom which helped my parents cover the college expenses of their kids. They watched all five of us graduate from the University of Missouri without going into debt.

At the time, I didn't dwell on my parents' amazing accomplishment, but as I contemplated how my husband and I were going to cover the college costs of our son and daughter, I marveled at their feat. Actually, my mom and dad not only made sure that I had the opportunity to get a college degree, they also indirectly helped me figure out how to duplicate what they had done on a smaller scale. My parents instilled in me a love of learning, which has provided me with a strong desire to explore subjects that fascinated me. College became one of those subjects.

I also feel fortunate that I have been able to share what I've learned over the years with the people who have discovered my blog—TheCollegeSolution.com. I have learned a great deal from the parents and teenagers who spend time at my blog.

I also want to thank three experts in the higher-ed field for reviewing some of my book chapters and making valuable suggestions. Mark Kantrowitz, the publisher of FinAid and Fastweb, reviewed my financial chapters while Bob Schaeffer of FairTest: National Center for Fair & Open Testing looked over my test-optional chapter. I am grateful to Dr. Karen Weaver, director of athletics at Penn State Abington and a nationally recognized expert on collegiate athletics, for reviewing my sports scholarship chapter. I also want to thank Paula Bishop, a CPA in Bellevue, Washington, who is a go-to person for me when I have tricky financial aid questions.

I've reserved my biggest thank you to my husband, Bruce, and our children, Ben and Caitlin, for all the support they gave me while I was rewriting this book. They can tell you that it's not easy living with me when I'm in the midst of a book project. And finally, I can't forget Minerva, our golden retriever, who kept me company through every line of this book.

Lynn O'Shaughnessy
TheCollegeSolution.com

About the Author

Lynn O'Shaughnessy is a nationally recognized higher-ed author, journalist, and speaker. She writes frequently about college issues for *CBS MoneyWatch* and for her own popular college blog at TheCollegeSolution.com.

Lynn has written or been interviewed about college for such media outlets as *Money Magazine, Bloomberg Businessweek, The New York Times, Wall Street Journal, Los Angeles Times, Fox Business News, Huffington Post, Parade Magazine, CBS This Morning, USA Today*, and *US News & World Report*. She is the consulting director of college planning, K-12, at the University of California, San Diego Extension. She also is a frequent speaker on how families can find and afford great schools. Lynn's daughter is a recent college graduate and her son is a college sophomore. Lynn is a graduate of the University of Missouri's School of Journalism.

Introduction

For many years, I was a financial journalist who wrote for such national media outlets as *Forbes*, *The Wall Street Journal*, and *BusinessWeek*. I thought that I had covered just about every financial topic imaginable until I realized that I had overlooked one subject.

My daughter Caitlin was in high school when it occurred to me that I knew nothing about what families can do to make college more affordable once their days of saving for this big-ticket item are over. How do parents take what they have managed to accumulate for college and stretch the cash as far as possible?

I began thinking a lot about college costs when Caitlin's initial plan for college no longer struck me as feasible. My bright, outgoing daughter had assumed that she would attend the University of California, Berkeley, which was her dad's alma mater, but by her sophomore year in high school, we realized that Berkeley wasn't a realistic choice because she would have had to be near the very top of her class at her highly competitive high school. While paying for a UC school would have been more doable financially, we were faced with finding a Plan B.

While I was pondering all this, someone suggested that I buy a copy of a book titled *Colleges That Change Lives: 40 Schools That Will Change the Way You Think About Colleges* by Loren Pope, who long ago was the education editor of *The New York Times* and later became an independent college counselor. I remember reading the slim book, which had become a classic, at my son's soccer tournament in the high desert of Southern California. I was mesmerized by Pope's loving description of seemingly delightful colleges that I didn't even know existed. College of Wooster? Evergreen State? Agnes Scott College?

Reading the book prompted me to wonder if Caitlin should expand her search to schools beyond state universities in California. Half of all college freshmen attend schools that are no more than a two-hour drive away from home, while just 14% venture at least 500 miles away, but my daughter was game to explore promising schools wherever they might be.

While Caitlin was excited about casting a wider net for college, I wondered if distant schools—particularly private ones—would be prohibitively expensive. To answer this question, it helped to be a financial journalist. I began writing magazine articles that addressed how families with teenagers can shrink the cost of college, which allowed me to talk to knowledgeable insiders. Uppermost in my mind were questions like these:

- Who qualifies for financial aid?
- Who earns scholarships?
- Are schools as expensive as they seem?

What I really wanted to know, however, is whether Caitlin could claim a share of the billions of dollars available for families to pay for college.

I was heartened by what I learned. I discovered that students don't have to be at the top of their class to attract the interest of the vast majority of schools. Teenagers certainly don't need 4.0 grade point averages to earn scholarships from state and private colleges and universities. In fact, I discovered that at a surprising number of schools, nearly every student receives some type of price cut.

As we toured schools, Caitlin became excited about attending a liberal arts college, which you'll learn more about in this book. She received scholarship offers from several colleges, but ultimately ended up choosing between Juniata College and Dickinson College, which are both lovely schools in central Pennsylvania. She selected Juniata, and after four great years—including two semesters at the University of Barcelona in Spain—she graduated and experienced no problem finding a phenomenal job back home in San Diego.

After Caitlin departed for college, I could have returned to writing about mutual funds, Treasury bonds, retirement planning, and other topics that I used to routinely cover. I decided, however, to ditch all that and focus on the issues that petrify parents who aren't sure how they can possibly handle the cost of college. In 2008, I started my blog, The College Solution (www.thecollegesolution.com), which now contains years' worth of advice on paying for college and selecting the right schools. I also write a college blog for CBS MoneyWatch, and for awhile I also wrote one for *US News & World Report*. And, of course, I wrote the first edition of *The College Solution: A Guide for Everyone Looking for the Right School at the Right Price*.

I eagerly switched gears to focus on college issues because they continue to get short shrift from the very people who should be helping families. Financial journalists, for instance, routinely write articles for parents with young children about the need to begin saving early for college, but they rarely provide guidance for the millions of parents with teenagers who haven't saved enough.

Journalists' failings are small potatoes compared to the shortcomings of the financial industry. It's rare to find financial advisers who possess even a rudimentary understanding of college financing. (And I'm not talking about the tiny minority of ethically challenged guys who urge parents to move their money around to avoid detection from financial aid formulas. Stay away from them!)

I believe the primary reason why the financial industry isn't educating families on college issues is because there isn't enough money in it to make it worthwhile. The industry's focus is on retirement because that's where the big bucks are. You will find a lot of advice on the websites of brokerage firms about how Americans can stretch their retirement account assets once they need the money, but I've yet to find one of these sites that provides advice about stretching college dollars.

I was even more surprised by the lack of knowledge among high school counselors, who are the go-to source for millions of families. I've met few parents who are pleased by the college advice that they are receiving from their children's high school counselors. As you'll learn later in the book, these counselors are routinely required to earn master's degrees in counseling to qualify for their positions, but the nation's schools of education shamefully ignore college issues in the curriculum.

While I started out focused chiefly on the finances of college, I also became fascinated by the different types of academic choices that teenagers face. When I give talks, I often ask the parents and students in the audience if they know the difference between a college and a university. It's rare that even a single person raises his or her hand. One of my chief aims in writing this second edition of *The College Solution* is to help students decide what type of schools are best for them and to also consider overlooked academic gems.

By the time it was my son Ben's turn to explore colleges, our family was in an even better position to evaluate schools both academically and financially. After seeing the kind of experience that his sister had at a liberal arts college, Ben also chose that path. After visiting about ten liberal arts colleges, Ben picked Beloit College in Wisconsin, where he's currently majoring in art and math. When my daughter asked Ben, halfway through his freshman year, what he thought about his school, he replied, "I love Beloit more than life itself." That was an amazing statement particularly coming from my son, a pretty cynical kid who usually has no use for hyperbole.

I figured that my husband and I saved about $125,000 off the sticker price of our son and daughter's college educations, and just as importantly, they both picked schools where they could grow academically. I wrote this second edition of *The College Solution* so you too can become an empowered consumer and accomplish much the same thing with your children.

Part I

Shrinking the Cost of College

1

Making College More Affordable

Colleges have gotten increasingly good at price discriminating. The list price is set high, and then many customers are offered a discount called "financial aid" based on their ability to pay. Here's the secret plan: In the future, Harvard will cost $1 billion a year, and only Bill Gates's children will pay full price. When anyone else walks through the door, the message will be "special price, just for you."

—Greg Mankiw, professor of economics at Harvard University

One of the curious aspects of how colleges price their bachelor's degrees is that students pay different prices for the same education. Colleges essentially price themselves like airline tickets.

A person who books a flight on United Airlines at 11 p.m. on a Tuesday might pay $50 less than a fellow passenger who waits until waking up on Wednesday to make the reservation. We know the airlines have their reasons for their price fluctuations, but heck if we know what their motivations are.

College pricing can be just as mysterious. The prices families pay can vary significantly and, on its face, make as much sense as an airline charging more money for reservations made within hours or minutes of each other. (I've even had airlines boost their fares while I was in the middle of making a reservation.)

The students who enjoy the cheaper prices aren't always the most deserving. It's not always the brightest students or the most financially needy teenagers who receive the biggest awards. You can have two equally smart students whose families make the exact same income and own houses with the identical equity, and one might end up paying full fare while the other enjoys the blue-light special price.

The best way to increase your family's chances of capturing a price cut is to understand the motivation behind the pricing discrimination that routinely happens behind closed doors on college campuses. When money is limited, and it is for nearly all institutions of higher education, colleges and universities do play favorites with their applicants.

Beyond the colleges' own pricing practices, financial aid formulas also pick winners and losers. Not all families who hope to win at what they often perceive to be a financial aid lottery are treated equally. You can blame a lot of that on politics. Student aid experts aren't the ones in charge of the methodology that most schools use to determine how much aid individual students will receive. Congress oversees the system, which explains a lot.

In the next 14 chapters, you will get an inside peek on why the system rewards some students and leaves others with staggering debt. More importantly, you will learn what you can do to make college as affordable as possible for your family.

So let's get started.

Action Plan

You'll enjoy a greater chance of cutting the cost of college if you understand how colleges price their bachelor's degrees.

2

Show Me the Money

Among the elite private schools, tuition is driven by what the market will bear. It's that simple. They charge a higher tuition because they can.

—Edward R. Fiske, author of *Fiske Guide to Colleges*

When teenagers are looking for colleges, the price is often not something they think much about.

That's why I wasn't surprised when a mom told me about the experience of her daughter's boyfriend, who was thrilled to get an acceptance letter from the University of Notre Dame.

The teenager, who was a phenomenal student, was shocked at how little money Notre Dame gave him to defray the cost. The future journalism major was even more worried because his parents weren't going to provide much financial help to this young man, who now assumed he will have to juggle multiple campus jobs with a tough course load and graduate with an excessive amount of debt.

While money was an issue, the teenager had never researched whether he had a realistic chance of receiving any sort of price discount from Notre Dame. Some pricey schools are more generous than others. The teenager had also never considered less expensive alternatives. For instance, the University of Missouri, which has one of the finest journalism schools in the country, charges a fraction of the price. The mother, however, noted that the teenager was only interested in "prestige" schools.

Many of you, I'm sure, can relate to this student's dream of attending Notre Dame. Who wouldn't want to boast about graduating from a brand-name institution that makes others envious? But the glow of attending a nationally prestigious school will surely fade when a graduate is overwhelmed by student debt and wondering if he'll be eating Cheerios for dinner on a regular basis.

What this cautionary story illustrates is this: At the start of the college search process, parents and teenagers need to appreciate what kind of help they can realistically expect from not only colleges, but also from other potential sources of financial assistance. Knowing where the money is located can help narrow the hunt to realistic college choices. And by realistic, I don't always mean those with the cheapest price tags. Some of the most expensive schools in the country can actually be the most affordable for the right students.

The Largest Sources of College Cash

So where exactly are all those billions of college dollars stashed?

As you can see, from the table, the federal government represents the largest source of grants (free money) and colleges are the No. 2 source.

Scholarships/Grant Sources	Percentage of All Grant Aid
Federal government	44%
Colleges	36%
State government	9%
Private scholarships	6%

The majority of college students will receive grants from at least one of these sources. What's important to understand is which of these sources do you have a realistic chance of tapping into. Let's take a look at all four of them.

Federal Government Grants

Household income is what makes or breaks a family's chances for federal help. To qualify for federal grants, your family has to be struggling financially.

The big daddy of all federal grants is the Pell Grant. The maximum grant can change annually, but the top award for the 2013-2014 school year is $5,635—admittedly, not a princely sum.

More than two-thirds of students who qualify for the Pell Grant have families living within 150% of the poverty line. As a practical matter, to qualify for the full Pell Grant, families must have an adjusted gross income of less than $23,000. About a quarter of the remaining families making under $50,000 qualify for a smaller Pell award.

Even if you won't qualify for a federal grant, you will be eligible for federal college loans. Federal student loans are the superior choice for borrowers. To qualify for parent and student federal loans, you must complete the Free Application for Federal Student Aid (FAFSA), which you'll learn about later.

Institutional Awards

Private and state colleges and universities routinely provide grants to students of all income levels. The average grants at private institutions are especially high. Recently, the typical student at a private institution received grants that equaled a tuition discount of 49.1%, according to the National Association of College and University Business Officers. At a school where the tuition is $36,000, for example, a 49.1% price break would drop the tuition to $18,324. These grants, by the way, are not reserved solely for the brainiest of applicants. About 88% of students attending private schools receive some type of award.

As you'll learn, there are a variety of reasons why private schools often cut their prices as aggressively as stores on December 26. One prime motivator is this reality: Private institutions must compete with less expensive state institutions, which is where the majority of students attend. What many families don't realize is that the price gap between private and public schools has been narrowing in recent years as state support of public universities has shrunk and private schools have scrambled to maintain or even increase their financial aid levels. Because of the proliferation of grants, private schools can cost the same or less than a public university for some students.

Private colleges and universities also use grants to compete against each other. The competition for talented students (and not just those 4.0 students) is actually fierce and in conflict with the stubborn conventional wisdom that the majority of schools reject most students. That's untrue. Actually, only a small fraction of schools reject most of their applicants.

Like their private counterparts, state universities provide grants to students who need financial help, as well as wealthy teenagers. State grants typically aren't as high, but then the published price tags aren't as steep either. The percentage of students receiving grants also tends to be much lower than at private schools.

According to a study by The Education Trust, state institutions award at least half of merit awards to affluent students. At the typical state flagship university, which is the premiere public university in each state, half of the money goes to well-off students. The percentage rises to 55% at other public universities.

State universities dispense awards to affluent students for the same reason that their private peers do. They are jostling for top students to help boost their own reputations. Both state and private schools use grants to attract students, which they hope will help them inch up *US News & World Reports'* rankings or at least prevent them from slipping to a lower rung. This focus on attracting rich teenagers has created a situation where student bodies at some flagships are more affluent than at expensive private universities. The phenomenon, prompted Kati Hancock, president of The Education Trust, to comment, "It's almost as if some of America's best public colleges have forgotten that they are, in fact, public."

State Government Grants

States routinely award money to college students, but often the states impose formulas that hand out grants based on such factors as standardized test scores, grade point averages, and class ranks.

Some states restrict their grants to low- and middle-income students, while other merit-based programs are also open to wealthy teenagers who meet the academic standards. These latter programs have been particularly popular in the South and have attracted criticism for using limited state funds for students who don't need the help.

You shouldn't assume that state grants are available only for students who will be attending in-state public universities. In some states, such as California, residents can use the grants to help pay for private schools within their borders.

To learn more about these public grant programs, contact your state higher education agency. You can find the contact information for your state by Googling the terms "state higher education agencies" and "gov."

Private Scholarships

Many families mistakenly believe that private scholarships—those sponsored by nonprofit organizations, foundations, and companies—represent the most lucrative source of cash. These scholarships, however, represent the tiniest source of money, and yet that's where many students focus their hunt.

Because the federal government requires a college to consider outside private scholarships when calculating financial aid awards, these scholarships can actually reduce a student's aid package. Because of this reality, private scholarships can be a bigger benefit to affluent students. You'll learn more about private scholarships in Chapter 10, "Capturing Private Scholarships."

Action Plan

When exploring ways to reduce the cost of college, make sure you are looking in the right places. The four main sources are federal and state governments, private scholarships, and the colleges themselves.

3

The Colleges with the Best Financial Aid

Higher education in America is a big business. The college is trying to get you to pay the most money: you are trying to pay the least amount. It can be very costly to assume that the college is going to show you how to get the most aid.

—Kalman A. Chany, financial aid consultant and author of *Paying for College Without Going Broke*

An easy way to get a sense of whether a school is going to be generous to families who require financial aid is to look at the institution's *US News & World Report* rankings.

I'm not kidding. High rankings and gold-plated financial aid practices are the higher-ed industry's equivalent of pancakes and syrup. You won't find one without the other nearby. The schools at or near the top of the rankings heap are rich institutions with enough dough to underwrite the education of any middle-class or poor teenagers who are lucky enough to get in.

The institutional winners of the college rankings bonanza are so generous with their students that many of them don't even stuff loans into their financial aid packages. This magnanimous practice became de rigueur among elite schools in late 2007 and early 2008 before the stock market tanked. There are roughly six dozen so-called *no-loan* schools in the country, and the bulk of them are clustered on the East Coast.

The schools that award the most generous need-based financial aid packages include such universities as Brown, Columbia, Cornell, and California Institute of Technology, as well as elite liberal arts colleges such as Middlebury, Swarthmore, Haverford, and Pomona. A brilliant teenager whose parents make $60,000 annually will go to a school like Amherst or MIT for practically free. The trick for students of modest means is not how to pay for schools like Vassar and Williams colleges (the price will be a bargain for them), but how to get admitted since these schools reject the vast majority of their applicants.

The financial aid policies of the rest of the nation's colleges and universities are a mixed bag. Fat endowments aren't propping up these schools, and they don't enjoy the high concentrations of wealthy students that mob the most prestigious schools. Some of these institutions perform an admirable job of meeting a large percentage of the financial need of many their students. Other schools, however, are more interested in attracting affluent families by offering them attractive merit scholarships, while they play scrooge to everybody else by dispensing lousy financial aid packages.

Top-ranked public universities can be just as interested in attracting smart, well-off teenagers as their private peers, and they devote considerable money to attract this demographic. As a practical matter, however, most students attend nonselective state universities, which are fairly inexpensive to all comers.

Behind-the-Scenes: Enrollment Managers

What's fascinating is the motivation behind a school's decision on which applicants capture a price break and which don't. I can't delve into this topic without at least mentioning this fact: Private and public colleges and universities routinely employ in-house enrollment managers or hire consultants who devise ways for colleges to use their institutional cash as strategically as possible to assemble their freshman classes. Typically this means helping institutions leverage their own revenue to attract the kind of teenagers they covet. Enrollment management practices have turned financial aid from primarily a utilitarian way to help disadvantaged students into a powerful tool to attract high-achieving students and the wealthy.

The role of enrollment managers is controversial in higher-ed circles, but families have no knowledge that these practices even exist.

Matthew Quirk wrote the best article that I've seen on enrollment management in *The Atlantic* magazine way back in 2005. The article was such an eye opener for me that I remember where I was when I was reading it (on a plane). You can read the article by Googling its title, "The Best Class Money Can Buy."

Prestigious Schools and Rich Students

The schools blessed with the most prestigious brand names enjoy an advantage that thousands of other schools don't. They can charge full price to wealthy students. Rich parents will happily write checks totaling more than $250,000 in return for bragging rights to a school like Harvard. Consequently, a brilliant wealthy student hoping to get a merit scholarship from institutions like Yale University or MIT or Wellesley College can forget about it. It's not going to happen.

What is a more common practice among highly elite private research universities and liberal arts colleges is to dispense tiny merit awards to a fairly small group of wealthy students. Stanford and Northwestern universities and Carleton and Bowdoin colleges are among the top 10 colleges and universities in *US News'* rankings that provide token grants. When I checked, here was the average merit award for a wealthy child attending these schools: Bowdoin ($1,000), Carleton ($3,368), Northwestern ($2,521), and Stanford ($4,985).

Rich Schools and Poor Students

Elite institutions, which provide little to no money to truly wealthy students, explain that they adopted this stance because they reserve their institutional money for the students who truly require assistance. This certainly sounds noble, but there can be a disconnect between official policy and what's really going on.

The majority of these schools have not instituted admission preferences for poor teenagers, making it difficult for these students to get in. What's commonly used to measure the number of needy students at a school is the percentage of its Pell Grant recipients. Low- and lower middle-income students qualify for this federal money.

When I checked the percentage of Pell Grant recipients at the Ivy League schools, Princeton's percentage was the lowest (10%) while Columbia's (16%) was the highest. Just for fun, let's compare those statistics to two elite public institutions, the University of California, Berkeley, and UCLA, where 24% and 26% of the students are low income.

In 2011, *The Chronicle of Higher Education,* the leading industry publication, examined the number of low-income students attending the 50 schools with the highest endowments. Among these wealthy institutions, 15% of students were low income versus 26% of students attending state and other private colleges and universities. The wealthiest schools with the smallest percentage of poor students in 2008-2009, in order, were:

1. Washington University (St. Louis)
2. Harvard University
3. University of Virginia
4. University of Pennsylvania
5. Duke University
6. University of Notre Dame
7. University of Richmond
8. Yale University
9. Boston College
10. Princeton University

Elite institutions have deservedly received flak from higher-ed insiders who complain that they are making half-hearted efforts to find talented, low-income students. In a scathing essay, Daniel F. Sullivan, president emeritus of St. Lawrence University in Canton, New York, made this observation: "The wealthiest colleges and universities—those that can best afford the financial aid necessary to enroll a large number of low-income students—in fact enroll the smallest percentage of such students."

So what's the hang-up with these rich schools? These institutions are highly invested in remaining über elite, and that means continuing to be magnets for rich Americans. As a rule, the students with the highest test scores and grade point averages are wealthier students who are far more likely to attend excellent college prep high schools, benefit from SAT/ACT tutoring, participate in meaningful activities, and have college-educated parents who can motivate and guide them through the college admission process.

Motivation of Most Private Schools

Beyond the nation's most elite institutions, the vast majority of private colleges and universities provide merit awards to students of all income levels. It's easier to get into these schools—they aren't rejecting 80% or 90% of their applicants—but the financial aid awards are typically not as substantial as what you'd find at the impenetrable institutions. At these private schools, as well as state universities, most students are not going to get 100% of their financial need met.

These colleges and universities provide merit money to affluent students because frankly they have to offer carrots to attract them. While a wealthy teen's parents will underwrite a Princeton education because of the wow factor, parents are going to be less inclined to drop that kind of dough on a school like Beloit College in Wisconsin, which is the wonderful liberal arts college that my son Ben attends.

If Beloit College didn't offer a bright, affluent student a merit award, a teenager would be more likely to end up at a state university or one of the countless liberal arts colleges that do offer merit aid, including such Midwestern schools as Lawrence and Denison universities, as well as Macalester, Lake Forest, Wooster, Knox, Illinois Wesleyan, Coe, and St. Olaf colleges.

Beloit and most other private schools are considered "tuition driven." Without huge endowments to help defray yearly expenses, they depend largely on their tuition revenue to pay the bills. In a complicated balancing act, they need enough affluent students, who will often capture some type of price break, to help cover the costs of the less fortunate students who are hoping for tremendous help.

Admission and financial aid officers must decide issues like this: Should we give four rich kids from the suburbs each a $10,000 merit award to seal the deal or reserve that $40,000 for one really poor inner-city kid? At tuition-driven schools, affluent students are subsidizing the education of students of modest means because they are still paying considerably more than most of the student body.

Other Scholarship Factors

How much schools must pay in scholarships to attract desirable students of all income levels hinges on a lot of factors. Geography is one. In general, I've found that universities located in East Coast cities tend to be less generous than schools where cows outnumber students. Kids dream about attending schools in cities like Boston, New York, Philadelphia, and Washington, DC, so the aid offers from these schools—beyond the most elite—can be underwhelming. I cringe when I hear students who need considerable financial aid say that they want to go to schools like Emerson College and NYU, Drexel, Fordham, St. Joseph's, American, and Northeastern universities.

Rankings ambitions also play a factor. Some schools must cough up more money to attract smart and/or affluent students who may be able to help boost a school's rankings. I'm using the following three universities in Washington, DC, to illustrate this phenomenon. Next to each name is the school's *US News'* ranking in the national university category:

- Georgetown University 22
- George Washington University 50
- American University 82

Keeping the rankings in mind, which school do you think gives the largest merit awards?

If you guessed American University, you were right. The average award for a freshman was $19,686 a year, which would bring the total award to $78,744. The merit scholarships from George Washington, which enjoys a better ranking, weren't as good. The typical recipient received a $14,530 per year award for a total of $58,120.

And what about Georgetown, which enjoys the highest college ranking of the trio? Here is Georgetown's average merit award: $0. Georgetown doesn't give money to students who have no real financial need because it doesn't need to. Wealthy students are eager to attend the Jesuit institution without a price break.

Action Plan

Low- and middle-income families should aim for schools that give out excellent financial aid packages.

If you're wealthy and you can't afford to pay full price or don't want to, you should look for colleges that would reward you with merit scholarships. Most schools fall into the category.

4

Who Gets Financial Aid?

This (financial aid) formula that purports to show you how much you can responsibly spend is produced by the federal government, which has the largest debt in the history of the world. It's like asking Cher how much plastic surgery you can have before it looks tacky.

—Zac Bissonnette, author of *Debt-Free U*

How rich is too rich to qualify for financial aid?

A mother who is a judge and a Harvard graduate once asked me that question. She and her husband make a good living—much better than good actually—and their son attends a private high school. She doesn't feel like she's wealthy enough to underwrite an exorbitantly expensive college education, but she wonders if colleges will lump her family into that too-rich-to-help category.

The judge's question is an excellent one because the kind of colleges and universities that families should target varies depending on whether the parents qualify for need-based financial aid. A straightforward way to determine your eligibility for financial aid is to determine your Expected Family Contribution or EFC.

If you apply for financial aid, you will receive your own EFC. Actually, you could end up with more than one, depending on what types of schools are on your list. Your EFC is a dollar figure that represents the amount of money that a college will expect your family to pay, at a minimum, for one year of schooling. This number tips off schools, as well as the federal and state governments, to whether you will need their help in covering the college tab.

Your EFC is generated by a variety of factors, but the most important one is the family's yearly income. Parents with large incomes generate higher EFC numbers while families that are barely scrapping by possess far lower ones. The smaller the EFC, the more likely that a college will offer a student need-based financial aid.

Other variables that can shrink or inflate your EFC include your taxable assets, the number of children in college at once (more is better), the age of the oldest parent (the older the better), and the marital status of a student's parents.

Expected family contributions can be as low as $0. You'll most commonly see a student with this EFC if the family earns less than $23,000. Just because a student's EFC is zero, however, usually doesn't mean that his college costs will be nonexistent either. Most low-income students will have to take out loans. Ideally, though, a child who has a low EFC will pay little for a college education.

On the other extreme, there is no EFC cap for wealthy Americans. I once talked with a father who was a corporate executive, whose EFC was $108,000. According to the financial aid formula, the father and his wife had the ability to pay $108,000 for their daughter's college costs for *one* year. Obviously, no college costs that much—at least not yet.

What the mother who is a judge shouldn't automatically assume is that her son wouldn't qualify for financial aid. The financial aid formulas are studded with quirky provisions that make it difficult to rule anything out until she is in possession of her own family's EFC.

A lot of experts have rightfully complained that the methodology used to generate EFC figures for millions of families is flawed. A family's EFC isn't always going to be fair. In fact, it's likely that the EFC won't pinpoint what a family can truly afford for college. And it's no wonder. Congress, rather than financial aid experts, mandates what's in the EFC's secret sauce.

The formula does play favorites. The methodology, for instance, favors homeowners, aggressive retirement savers, small business owners, some teenagers of divorce, and rural Americans. Let's take a look at some of these categories:

Home ownership. Parents who own expensive houses, particularly on each coast, worry that they will be rejected for financial aid because of their home equity. The federal formula, however, doesn't even ask if a family owns a primary residence. You could have paid cash for a stunning property in Palo Alto, California; Chevy Chase, Maryland; or the Upper Eastside in Manhattan, and it wouldn't hurt your aid chances.

Cost of living. The federal methodology doesn't take into consideration the cost of living, which penalizes families living in expensive cities or states. A family making $75,000 in Honolulu, which is the highest priced housing market in the country (a median home sells for $580,000), is expected to be able to cover college costs the same as someone living in Youngstown, Ohio, which is the nation's cheapest major housing market (a median house costs $55,000).

Retirement accounts. The federal EFC formula also doesn't care about the amount of money a family has stashed away in retirement accounts. You could have millions of dollars sitting in these retirement accounts and it wouldn't impact your aid award.

Small business. A family that owns a business with less than 100 full-time employees doesn't have to divulge its net worth.

Divorce. The federal formula penalizes married couples. If the Harvard mom was divorced and her ex-husband was a schoolteacher who made significantly less money than her, it's possible that her child could qualify for significant need-based financial aid. If the judge and the schoolteacher were married, however, it's unlikely they would qualify for any need-based financial aid.

The federal financial aid formula only inquires about the finances of the custodial parent. For financial aid purposes, the custodial parent is the one whose residence the child lived at for more than 50% of the year from the date the financial aid form is filed. Let's assume the judge is divorced. If her child lived with her 5 1/2 months and the dad 6 1/2 months, the father would fill out the federal aid application and would never even be asked about his ex-wife's salary or assets. If the custodial parent remarries, the new spouse's income and assets would also be used in financial aid calculations.

Child planning. Families sending twins or triplets to colleges are huge winners. The EFC drops considerably when more than one child is in college simultaneously. The EFC drops roughly 50% when two children are in school, and it shrinks even more with three college students. For instance, let's say a family's EFC was $30,000 when one child was in college, but the next year another starts as well. The EFC for each child would drop to about $15,000, which could qualify the students for significantly more financial aid.

There is no break, however, for families whose children are spaced four or more years apart. Thanks to the idiosyncrasies of the financial aid formula, parents who have one child in college at a time could end up paying far more than the parents who spaced their children closer together.

What Do You Do with Your EFC?

Your EFC by itself won't reveal your eligibility for financial aid. Another step is necessary. You'll need to compare your EFC with a school's so-called *cost of attendance*. Schools define their cost of attendance differently. Some calculate it as the cost of tuition and room and board. Some institutions also add the expense of books, transportation, and personal expenses.

Schools use the difference between a family's EFC and the cost of attendance to determine what the household's *demonstrated financial need* is. How much assistance a family may qualify for can be dramatically different if the school is low cost versus expensive.

Suppose, for instance, that you are a middle-income family and your EFC is $15,000. The in-state school that your child plans to attend is $13,000. You would not qualify for need-based aid because the school is cheaper than what your EFC indicates that you can afford to pay. Now let's assume that your child wants to attend a school that costs $40,000. You could end up with a package that includes $25,000 in financial aid. I got this figure by subtracting the EFC of $15,000 from the $40,000 price tag.

A Different EFC

Up to now, I've shared characteristics of the federal EFC formula, but there is another methodology that a far smaller number of families need to know about. An additional EFC will be calculated for families that complete the CSS/Financial Aid PROFILE, which is the financial aid application that 249 mostly private schools use in addition to the FAFSA.

The EFC that the PROFILE generates can be different because the application asks more questions and calculates aid differently. The PROFILE, for instance, takes into consideration the number of children in a household rather than how many are in college simultaneously. Most schools that use the PROFILE also want to know about a family's home equity and the finances of the noncustodial parent in cases of divorce. It also inquires about family businesses. The PROFILE often produces a higher EFC.

Schools that use the PROFILE can customize the application, so how schools deal with, for instance, divorce or a family's home equity varies. PROFILE schools, however, routinely put a cap on home equity that's tied to the household's yearly income, which keeps many families in the running for financial aid.

Action Plan

Your Expected Family Contribution may not be fair, but it is the number that colleges use to determine whether you will require financial help.

5

Winning the Educational Lottery

Six in ten families rule out some colleges because of sticker price, yet many do not know that the "net price" is typically far lower.

—Report from American Enterprise Institute for Public Policy Research

I crossed paths last year with a high school senior in St. Louis who dreamed of becoming a doctor. John earned excellent grades and was extremely active at his school and in his community, but he didn't think he had the resources to attend a top school. His parents were divorced, and he was living with his mom, who made about $40,000 as a waitress.

I told John that he needed to apply to different types of colleges, including affordable state schools in Missouri, but I also said he should apply to expensive private colleges with excellent financial aid. One of the schools that I recommended was Grinnell College, a highly respected liberal arts college in Iowa.

I explained to John that getting into a school like Grinnell would be like winning the lottery. A student with a low Expected Family Contribution (EFC)—see the previous chapter for the definition—such as himself would have most of his tab covered. In fact, the private school would be more affordable than a state university.

Grinnell costs more than $50,000 a year, but the college promises to meet 100% of each of its student's *demonstrated financial need*. This means that after a family covers its EFC, the college will provide the rest in a financial aid package. If a family's EFC is $6,000, which is probably close to what John's EFC was, then the college's financial aid package would cover the remaining amount.

Only wealthy and prestigious colleges and universities with large endowments can meet 100% of *all* their students' demonstrated financial needs, and Grinnell belongs in that category. Warren Buffett happens to be a life trustee of Grinnell, and the college was an original investor in Intel, which was co-founded by Robert Noyce, a Grinnell alumnus.

When assembling a financial aid package, Grinnell and all other schools start with government money first. If the student is eligible for federal or state aid, the school puts those grants in the package. The school then kicks in its own institutional grants. Schools also include loans in their financial aid packages. The federal Stafford loan is the most popular loan that colleges include.

In Grinnell's case, nearly all of the financial aid that its students receive is grants. The typical Grinnell freshman requiring aid recently received grants worth $32,249. Believing students should have some skin in the game, the college includes a modest amount of *self-help* in the package. In the higher-ed world, self-help refers to loans and work-study jobs. Because of Grinnell's generous aid policy, the typical student who borrows for college leaves with just $15,720 in debt, which is well below the national average of roughly $25,000 for all four-year private and public schools.

If all schools were as generous as Grinnell, I probably wouldn't have needed to write this book. But in reality, most schools can't match this college's largess. In fact, there are probably only five dozen schools—out of thousands—that can do what Grinnell does.

New York University

To illustrate the financial aid policies of a school that isn't generous, I'm using New York University, because it is on the dream list of many teenagers.

NYU was recently charging about $57,000 for tuition and room/board. The popular school, however, only meets 69% of its typical freshman's demonstrated financial need, which is low for a highly selective university. NYU is well-known in higher-ed circles for its poor financial aid.

The federal government has calculated that NYU's net price (what you pay after grants are deducted) makes it the nation's 15th most expensive private university. Many of the schools that are even more expensive are music conservatories and art schools such as the Boston Conservatory, Pratt Institute, and the Rhode Island School of Design. (You can find the federal lists of the most expensive state and private schools in the country by Googling the term *"College Affordability and Transparency Center."*)

Now let's see what NYU's aid practices would have meant for John's family with their estimated EFC of $6,000. Just counting room/board and tuition, the family would need $51,000 in assistance, but the aid package would fall short. Using the average 69% figure, the family would get a package worth $35,190, but a chunk of that would be would be loans. The latest statistics that I could find show that loans and work/study jobs represent 38% of NYU's typical package.

According to financial aid statistics on the College Board, NYU's average need-based grant was recently just $21,348 versus Grinnell's $32,249, which is a less expensive school.

And what about the average debt that NYU grads incur? The scary figure is $41,300. What's also worrisome is a figure that NYU keeps secret—the number of students that have their full financial need met. According to the latest available statistics, 2,763 freshmen received financial aid, but NYU withheld the number of these students who had their full need met. In contrast, Grinnell covered the full need of 100% of its freshmen.

NYU boasts that roughly 70% of its freshmen receive financial aid, but that is a meaningless statistic. What's important is how NYU or any other school treats the students who qualify for financial aid.

Finding Your Own Statistics

Your job is to find schools, based on your EFC, that will be as generous as possible and avoid those that will gladly educate your child, but leave you in serious debt after the graduation ceremony.

Clearly in the two examples that I shared, a school like Grinnell is the superior choice for a student who requires financial assistance.

It's actually not hard to measure the generosity of any school that interests you. Head to the College Board's BigFuture website (http://bigfuture.org), which is a destination for families wanting to learn more about finding and affording colleges. Type the name of the school into the search box. Once you reach the school's profile, click on its Paying tab. Some statistics will be displayed on this page while you will have to click another link—Policies & Stats—to access other figures.

Here are some of the statistics you will find:

- Number of students who were judged to have need.
- Number who were offered aid.
- Number who had full need met. (The higher the number the better.)
- Percentage of need met. (The higher the percentage the better.)
- Average financial aid package.
- Average need-based scholarship or grant. (The higher the better.)
- Average non-need based aid. (This is merit aid for rich students.)
- Average indebtedness at graduation. (Lower is better.)

You can also find these financial aid statistics at the website of COLLEGEdata, a helpful online resource underwritten by 1st Financial Bank. The site offers a few more statistics on individual schools than the College Board. To find a school's profile on COLLEGEdata's website click on the Search for Colleges hyperlink on the home page and type in the name of a school.

Action Plan

Regardless of what your EFC is, you should evaluate schools to see which would be most generous to your child.

The College Board and COLLEGEdata are helpful resources when researching financial aid statistics for individual schools.

6

Calculating Your Expected Family Contribution

I can tell you that the current formula for determining EFC has everything to do with political realities and nothing to do with the financial realities under which students and families live.

—Diane Auer Jones, former U.S. assistant secretary of post-secondary education

When parents ask me what schools will give their children a price break, I invariably ask them this question: Do you know what your Expected Family Contribution is?

Families can't possibly start searching for schools that will be affordable to them until they obtain this figure. In the previous two chapters, I explained why your EFC is a critical number, and now you'll learn how to discover your own.

Most people only learn what their EFC is after they have completed the Free Application for Federal Student Aid (FAFSA). This is the federal application that families must complete if they desire financial aid or if they want to take advantage of federal college loans. (You can find the FAFSA application at www.fafsa.ed.gov.)

After a parent submits the federal application electronically, he or she receives a prompt notification of what the household's EFC is while still on the federal website. Waiting until you complete the financial aid application, however, is far too late in the game to be retrieving this important figure.

You should possess this number even before your child has drawn up his or her college list.

If you apply exclusively to state universities and colleges, you should end up with one EFC. Students who also apply to private schools, however, could possess more than one EFC. The reason for multiple numbers is because schools can use different EFC methodologies to allocate their own institutional grants.

Where to Find EFC Calculators

The calculator that I like to use is at the website of the College Board's BigFuture (http://bigfuture.org.). The federal government also offers its own EFC calculator, which is called the FAFSA4caster. The FAFSA4caster, which you can find by Googling the term, calculates financial aid based only on the federal methodology. The federal formula is used to determine whether a family is eligible for federal money such as Pell Grants and subsidized Stafford loans, as well as state grants.

If you want to use the College Board's calculator, head to its website and type "EFC calculator" into the search box in the upper right-hand corner. The calculator asks whether you want to use the federal methodology or the institutional methodology or both.

The vast majority of colleges and universities use only the federal methodology, which is tied to the FAFSA. About 250 selective and almost entirely private institutions also rely on the CSS/Financial Aid PROFILE, which uses the institutional methodology to determine which students deserve their in-house grants. All private and state schools use the FAFSA to determine student eligibility for federal and state assistance.

You'll want to try both methodologies because at this point you shouldn't limit your school choices. The EFC that each methodology produces can be different because the institutional formula drills deeper into a family's finances. The EFC the PROFILE generates can also vary by school because the institutions can customize their aid applications.

EFC Questions

An EFC calculator asks questions about the following:

- Family size
- Age of oldest parent
- Parents' marital status
- Number of students who will be in college
- Parents' adjusted gross income
- Student's income
- Home equity
- Income taxes paid for most recent calendar year
- Untaxed income/benefits
- Nonretirement investments
- Cash and savings

When playing with these calculators, remember that financial circumstances change. For example, if you used an EFC calculator when your daughter was in 10th grade and months later you lose your job, those figures will no longer be accurate. All the results will be estimates until you file for financial aid when your child is a senior in high school.

Action Plan

Don't wait until a child's senior year in high school to find out your Expected Family Contribution. Use an EFC calculator to get a ballpark figure long before you apply to any schools.

7

A Revolutionary Calculator

Net price calculators are going to be as revolutionary as US
News & World Report's *college rankings.*

—Kathy Dawley, president/CEO of Maguire Associates, a
higher-ed consulting firm

How much is a college going to cost me?

If you direct that question to an admission rep at a college fair or
during a campus visit, be prepared to hear something like this:

> *"If you're interested in our school, you should definitely apply.
> We have scholarships ranging from a few thousands dollars a
> year to full-rides.*

When families hear these encouraging words—or a variation of
them—they often become optimistic. *Wow! There's money for my
teenager at this school. Wouldn't it be great if she could get a full-ride
scholarship?*

There is a huge difference, however, between snagging a $4,000
scholarship and winning a full-ride that might be worth $200,000 or
more. Colleges, however, have not been keen on sharing the odds
about whether their institutions would give a teenager a token award
or a substantial package.

Frankly, many admission officers feel uncomfortable talking specifics about what a student might realistically expect in an aid package. Young, idealistic admission reps might not even know how the
money is doled out. As you'll read elsewhere in this book, some of the
financial-aid practices that schools rely on are not pretty and are kept
under wraps.

Because college prices have traditionally been anything but transparent, families have often treated college applications as if they were lottery tickets. Their children apply and then mom and dad keep their fingers crossed and hope for a big payoff months later when schools send out their admission letters and financial aid packages.

Sometimes families are relieved when the award letters arrive, but all too often they are disappointed, or even stunned, by modest (or worse) financial aid offers. By the spring when the financial aid notices often arrive, it's too late for do-overs. Application deadlines have typically long since passed, and schools are now expecting parents to put down deposits by May 1.

Families are then stuck with the choices in front of them, which can lead to decisions that are emotional and financially devastating. Parents wonder if they should raid their 401(k) or other retirement accounts to help pay for college. Teenagers, dazzled by the prospects of attending their dream schools, can be willing to sign any loan documents without ever thinking through the consequences of their impulsive wishes.

Using a Net Price Calculator

Admittedly, all this sounds bleak, but it's not. Families who are in the know now have a chance to judge the affordability of specific colleges long before financial aid letters are mailed. It's an exciting time for families with college-bound teenagers because schools can no longer hide behind vague promises of money.

You can credit this sea change to a tool called a *net price calculator*. These net price calculators can empower parents and teenagers to make informed decisions about which schools are going to be affordable and which are going to be budget busters. The calculators provide families who take advantage of them with a personalized estimate of what a particular school will cost them.

The calculators focus on the net price because that is the only figure that ultimately matters. The net price is what a family will pay after grants and scholarships—all free money—are deducted from a school's cost of attendance, which includes such things as tuition, room/board, and books. A calculator determines what grants the student would qualify for from the school itself, as well from the state and federal governments.

Let's say that a teenager applies to a college that costs $45,000 and receives a total of $20,000 in grants. The net price for this school would be $25,000.

All schools that participate in the federal financial aid program—and that covers nearly all institutions—have one of these calculators installed on their websites.

To use a net price calculator, a family needs to gather the latest income tax returns and investment account statements for the parents and teenager. Some calculators also inquire about a child's academic achievement by asking for a teen's grade point average, standardized test scores, class rank, and academic honors. Some schools delve further by inquiring about such things as community service and extra-curricular activities, including athletics, scouts, and leadership.

Net Price Calculator Accuracy

Unfortunately, not all calculators are equally helpful. Some calculators may be faulty because they are based on the federal government's template. The chief complaint about these particular calculators is that they are too simplistic because they don't ask enough questions to provide accurate information. The simplest calculator may pose just seven or eight questions.

In creating its calculator model, the federal government was trying to balance the need of families to obtain accurate price information while at the same time not scaring off parents who might be intimidated by a calculator that asks too many questions. Frankly, I think this fear is overblown. Even the most complicated calculator shouldn't take more than 15 to 20 minutes tops to complete. And what's 15 minutes compared to the enormity of what is at stake?

Private colleges and universities, as well as state flagship universities that attract a lot of students beyond their borders, are more likely to rely on custom-built calculators that require additional answers. There is a higher probability that these calculators are accurate.

How to Use the Calculators

What's the best way to use net price calculators? Don't wait until your child is sending off applications before you turn to these tools! Run the numbers long before your child reaches that stage. Using the calculators in advance will reduce the chance that a teenager will develop a list of colleges that are financially inappropriate. Getting financial verdicts at the beginning of your college search should cut down on tears later on.

Savvy consumers will want to try out different combinations of variables on these calculators to explore how they might be able to maximize their awards. For instance, a teen may use different SAT or ACT test scores to see whether a higher result would trigger a greater award. Based on the outcome, a teen might decide to retake a standardized test. Students could also check to see whether a different declared major or a grade point average would mean more money at a particular school. The questions that a calculator poses can provide hints to the types of factors that schools favor and reward financially.

Using aggregated net price data, it's only a matter of time before web-based outfits begin offering the same kind of information for college-bound students that Zillow, Carmax, and Expedia provide for people shopping for houses, cars, and travel. Imagine going to a website and plugging in numbers that allow you to see what colleges would offer your child the best package. That day is coming.

Playing Hide and Seek

While the net price calculator is a tremendous tool for families, plenty of schools aren't overjoyed by their use. In fact, many institutions appear to be hiding their calculators deep in the catacombs of their websites. These schools would prefer that families not even know that they exist.

It's not too tough to appreciate why some institutions are behaving this way.

Institutions that have historically offered mediocre financial aid are obviously not thrilled by the calculator requirement. If families armed with solid financial aid data start staying away from stingy schools, these institutions might have to reevaluate their financial priorities.

Schools are also worried about the engaged consumers who are busily running scenarios on the calculators in the hopes of capturing the best prices. There is also a fear among private colleges in particular that their competitors are using the calculators in an attempt to uncover their financial aid priorities. Imagine how paranoid Coca-Cola would be if PepsiCo was trying to uncover its soda recipes.

Action Plan

Not all calculators are accurate, particularly if the schools are using the federal template, but they should continue to improve.

If an outcome seems wildly different from the results using other calculators, double-check your numbers.

If you can't find a school's net price calculator, contact the school and ask for its location.

8

The Allure of Out-of-State Public Universities

As I watch my daughter start her college applications, I'm cringing inside because she wants to apply to out-of-state public schools such as UCLA, Georgia Tech, and Purdue. Although Purdue states that it does have scholarships for out-of-state students, I'm worried that this will end up being a waste of time and the cost of the application fees.

—Mom of a high school senior

An artistic teenager from New York City was excited when she got accepted at the University of Michigan, one of the nation's premiere flagships. She was even more jazzed about Michigan after she attended the school's summer orientation for the Class of 2015.

It was only after the teenager returned from Ann Arbor that her dad looked at the bill again. His daughter had received a $5,000-a-year scholarship from the school, which dropped the price to a reasonable $19,000. At least that's what the dad initially thought.

As it turned out, the $19,000 was for just *one* semester, not for the entire year. The father told me that he explained to his daughter that she could still go to her dream school, but it would be a financial stretch. She decided, however, to change her plans and enroll elsewhere.

I'm sharing this story because it illustrates one of the most prominent and controversial trends in public higher education. Across the country, tuition increases at state universities have been rising significantly higher than inflation. The rate of tuition hikes at state schools is also outpacing private colleges and universities. This is posing great hardships for low- and middle-income students who are discovering that their state flagship is becoming out-of-reach financially. Families whose teenagers want to attend public universities outside their own states, however, are experiencing the biggest sticker shock.

Across the country, public universities, and in particular the flagships, are in an all-out admission war to attract smart out-of-state students. Prestigious schools such as the University of Virginia, University of North Carolina, University of Wisconsin, UCLA, and the University of California at Berkeley have always been extremely popular with their homegrown talent, but these and many other state schools are welcoming a growing number of students from outside their borders.

The University of Arizona recently enrolled more freshmen from California than six campuses from the California State University system, according to an article in *The Chronicle of Higher Education*. Admission officials at the University of Oregon have joked that their school could be called the University of California at Eugene. The University of South Carolina has regional counselors who work full time in such states as Georgia, Texas, Ohio, and Pennsylvania.

Chasing Dollars

Why are out-of-state students such a commodity? There are a variety of explanations, but the No. 1 reason revolves around money.

You are no doubt aware that state governments have been reducing their support to public universities. It's probably been happening in your own state. In many cases, the financial commitment from state legislatures has been eroding for years, but the slippage became even more pronounced when the recession hit in the late 2000's.

One way that state universities have attempted to staunch the financial hemorrhaging is to aggressively recruit nonresidents in this country and overseas. To admission offices, students from elsewhere are gold because they typically pay two to three times more in tuition than residents. The tuition and room/board for nonresidents at the University of California campuses, for instance, exceeds $50,000. In comparison, Californians pay roughly $28,000.

Percentage of Students Who Are Nonresidents

Here is a sampling of flagships along with the percentage of undergraduates who are outsiders:

Indiana University	31%
University of Alabama	42%
University of Arizona	33%
University of California, Berkeley	30%
University of Colorado	43%
University of Iowa	49%
University of Michigan	38%
University of North Dakota	67%
University of Oklahoma	37%
University of Oregon	47%
University of South Carolina	36%
University of Vermont	75%
University of Virginia	29%
University of Wisconsin	37%

Not all flagships are heavy recruiters—only 8% of students at the University of Texas in Austin and the University of Illinois at Champagne-Urbana are from out of state, while just 3% of students at the University of Florida are—but it is a growing trend.

Fewer High School Graduates

Demographics are another reason why admission staffers at public universities have become road warriors. The college-age population in regions such as New England as well as parts of the Midwest and South is declining. The drop will become even steeper in some states in the next few years. Even more important for these schools is this reality: There will be fewer affluent high school grads with college-educated parents, which is the sweet spot for these schools. If there aren't enough homegrown prospects, schools hope to poach them from other states.

Chasing Prestige

Universities are also motivated by the desire to attain prestige or burnish their reputations through *US News & World Report's* college rankings. You might be surprised at this. After all, shouldn't a state university's main job be to educate its own children? Why should a state school care if a peer institution 600 miles away enjoys a better ranking?

Public universities, however, appear to be every bit as committed to inching up the rankings as private schools. And if that requires recruiting outside their borders, so be it. If brilliant students aren't naturally attracted to schools like the University of Alabama and the University of Oklahoma, then the institutions will roll out the cash awards. That's surely why, for instance, the University of Oklahoma was able to brag in a press release that its freshman class contained more National Merit Scholars than all but four schools: Harvard University, University of Chicago, University of Southern California, and Northwestern University.

Rich Student Favoritism

If you would like to attend an out-of-state university, your chances are greater than ever. A bright kid from New York or Minnesota who always dreamed of attending the University of California, Berkeley, now enjoys better odds. What families need to consider, however, is the cost. For many students, the price will be prohibitively expensive because of the extra costs state universities routinely slap onto the tab of outsiders.

Realistically, the students who can take advantage of the admission gold rush are wealthy families. The kinds of families who can write a $50,000-a-year check without jeopardizing their ability to gas up their cars and put food on the table. That might not bother you if you fit the description, but it does worry higher-ed insiders who have been concerned—even before the out-of-state gold rush—that state flagships are magnets for wealthy students.

The Education Trust, a nonprofit advocacy group that occasionally examines state flagship admission and financial aid practices, concluded in a recent report that the students who attend flagships are wealthier as a whole than students who attend the typical *private* college or university. Half of the merit scholarships that flagship universities dispense go to students who are too affluent to qualify for need-based aid.

This rich-kid favoritism is controversial. Detractors accuse the flagships of trying to privatize their institutions by rejecting their own teenagers, particularly in the low- and middle-income brackets, in return for wealthy outsiders.

It's indisputable that affluent students are a demographic that administrators have trained their sights on. A recent survey of hundreds of senior admission officers by *Inside Higher Ed*, a respected online trade publication, revealed that more than half of administrators at state universities said their *top* focus was attracting full-pay students to their campuses.

University administrators counter that the level of state support has shrunk so much that flagships deserve far more autonomy to decide whom they accept and how they set their tuition. The schools say they can be trusted to continue to do the right thing for their residents. I'm not sure about that.

Some skeptics have even questioned the financial need to recruit students outside their borders. To boost their argument toward privatization, state flagships point out that support from state governments has been shrinking for many years. Kevin Carey, a shrewd higher-ed observer and the Education Sector's policy director, suggests that the argument is disingenuous. The State Higher Education Executive Officers, according to Carey, determined that inflation-adjusted state spending per college student declined only $154 between 1985 and 2008, which is less than a tenth of 1%. What universities prefer to focus on is the state's reduced level of support as measured by the percentage of their entire budget. These percentages have dropped but it's because university spending has grown so rapidly.

Regardless of the naysayers, it's unlikely that the out-of-state recruiting trend will diminish.

Your Opportunity to Attend a Flagship

It would be wrong, however, to suggest that only rich students can afford out-of-state flagships. Some teenagers can capture a sizable price break from premiere state schools beyond their borders. The universities, however, typically reserve this money for their brightest applicants. Whether you qualify as one of those students depends largely on your statistics—grade point average, standardized test scores, and class rank.

State universities must process such a huge crush of applications that the admission offices can't spend time getting to know each applicant. They don't have the luxury of evaluating students holistically. Your numbers will have to do. And your numbers, frankly, must be stellar to qualify for serious money.

Here's an example: The University of Colorado was recently awarding $55,000 scholarships ($15,000 for the first two years, $12,500 for the second two years) for the top 1% to 3% of admitted nonresidents. A smaller $20,000 scholarship ($5,000 a year) is available to the top quarter of admitted nonresidents. The typical student who qualified for the less valuable scholarship recently earned a 3.85 GPA and an ACT score of at least 29 and a SAT score of 1300 or higher. Earning the top scholarship for nonresidents, however, isn't going to make Colorado cheap. Tuition and room/board for nonresidents at the Boulder flagship exceeds $42,000 a year.

Even if you are a valedictorian with perfect SAT scores, you won't qualify for merit scholarships at some state schools. Some public institutions don't provide merit awards to outsiders. Schools that fall into that category include the University of California campuses, University of Oregon, and the University of Washington.

Before you fall in love with a flagship in another state, research to see what kind of financial aid policy the school maintains for outsiders. You should be able to find this information on the school's admission pages. Perhaps an easier way to locate the information is to Google the name of the university along with "out-of-state scholarships."

Action Plan

While out-of-state flagship universities are popular with students, understand the costs before pursuing them.

9

Looking Across State Lines for a Bargain

No place has proved more popular with bargain-hunting non-residents than flat, cold, landlocked North Dakota.

—*Wall Street Journal* article

Can you imagine living in a state where the number of students graduating from high school is less than 7,400? If you can't, you must not live in North Dakota.

Don't snicker. The lack of students in the Peace Garden state can present you with an opportunity. Few teenagers include universities in North Dakota on their college dream lists, but maybe they should.

Schools that lack rankings mojo—and that is the majority of the nation's colleges and universities—have to try harder to attract students. Unlike elite public institutions that, in some cases, turn away the majority of their applicants, schools like those in North Dakota are working hard to attract students wherever they may live. One way that schools beneath the radar do this is to make it more affordable to attend.

Looking Where Others Aren't

In the previous chapter, you learned that prestigious state flagship universities can charge the equivalent of private school prices to non-residents, but far more state schools offer reasonable prices to bargain hunters. In the past, these public colleges and universities haven't advertised their affordable prices largely to avoid antagonizing state legislators who believe state schools should serve residents. Declining numbers of high school graduates in many states and the need to attract more tuition revenue—wherever schools can find it—has diminished the reticence to advertise their affordability.

The University of North Dakota and North Dakota State University provide examples of what public institutions will do to welcome outsiders to their campuses. The state of North Dakota, realizing it was facing a serious decline in high school students, poured money into its two research universities in hopes of attracting more out-of-staters. Blessed with oil money and the state's tradition of generously funding higher education, the universities have been able to keep their tuition low for everybody. The strategy worked, and nonresident enrollment has soared as students from places like New York, Florida, and California are moving to North Dakota for college.

Just heading to the cheapest schools, however, can be a recipe for trouble. You clearly need to evaluate the academics of any institution along with the price tag. Unfortunately, there are plenty of snobs who think that if a school isn't a brand name, it can't be any good. This, however, is ludicrous. The public universities in North Dakota, for instance, offer modest-sized classes that are taught by professors rather than graduate students or adjunct teachers. Prestigious flagships often can't promise their students the same.

A wide variety of public institutions scattered across the country offer bargain prices for nonresidents. For instance, the University of Minnesota at Morris, an excellent public liberal arts college, charges the same low tuition to Minnesotans and outsiders. The Fashion Institute of Technology, which is part of the State University of New York system, charges nonresidents less than $13,000 for tuition, which is unheard of for schools in Manhattan. Look around and you will find your own bargains.

Educational Compacts

Another way to cut the price of out-of-state public institutions is to see whether your state participates in an educational compact. Thanks to one of these agreements, you may pay the same price as a resident or capture a significant discount. There are regional compacts involving many states, as well as reciprocal agreements that border states honor.

States created some of these compacts after concluding that it was easier to piggyback off the offerings of institutions in other states rather than spend the money developing certain majors on their own.

The University of Kansas, for instance, operates an architecture school, but the University of Missouri does not. The University of Missouri system, however, maintains schools of dentistry and optometry, which KU does not. Consequently, dentistry and optometry students from Kansas can pay resident tuition at the University of Missouri, while Missouri students can enjoy the same deal when enrolled as architecture students at KU and Kansas State University.

The biggest compacts are regional in nature, and there are four of them. Some universities and colleges that participate in these regional compacts only accept students with particular majors. For instance, outsiders applying to the University of Oregon can apply through the compact if they are interested in less popular majors such as philosophy, medieval studies, music, math, art history, and some languages including French, Russian, Italian, and Japanese. Some schools require participants to have a certain grade point average and test scores to qualify.

Four Regional Compacts

Academic Common Market

Member states: Alabama, Arkansas, Delaware, Georgia, Kentucky, Louisiana, Maryland, Mississippi, Oklahoma, South Carolina, Tennessee, Virginia, and West Virginia. Florida, North Carolina, and Texas participate only through graduate programs.

Midwestern Higher Education Compact

Member states: Illinois, Indiana, Iowa, Kansas, Michigan, Minnesota, Missouri, Nebraska, North Dakota, Ohio, South Dakota, and Wisconsin.

New England Board of Higher Education

All 78 public colleges and universities participate in the tuition discount program offered in these six states: Connecticut, Maine, Massachusetts, New Hampshire, Rhode Island, and Vermont.

Western Undergraduate Exchange

Member states: Alaska, Arizona, California, Colorado, Hawaii, Idaho, Montana, Nevada, New Mexico, North Dakota, Oregon, South Dakota, Utah, Washington, and Wyoming.

You Must Ask

Don't expect schools to advertise their bargains for nonresidents. You have to do your own research. Request the reciprocal deal at the same time you apply to an out-of-state school.

Not all public schools in a state participate in these compacts. Often the most sought-after state universities don't. In the Western Undergraduate Exchange, for instance, UCLA, University of California, Berkeley, and the University of Washington don't belong to the compact. Schools that do include Colorado State University, Boise State University, University of Nevada, University of New Mexico, and the University of Montana.

Action Plan

There are a plenty of bargains for nonresidents at many state schools for those willing to do their own research. Look on the websites of the regional consortiums to see which schools offer reduced prices.

10

Capturing Private Scholarships

A wise student realizes that the vast majority of scholarships come from the colleges and universities themselves.

—College Venus blog

What is the best place to look for college cash?

If I asked that question to 100 high school students, I wouldn't be surprised if 99 of them responded with this answer: private scholarships.

A wide variety of groups sponsor private scholarships from service organizations like the Elks, Rotary, and Kiwanis clubs to alumni organizations, community foundations, and businesses. Corporations sponsor some of the best-known scholarships such as the Coca-Cola Scholars, Gates Millennium Scholars, and the Intel Science Talent Search. There are also private scholarships that elicit chuckles like the awards that go to left-handed students, teenagers who make awesome apple pies, and the couple who uses duck tape to create the coolest prom outfits.

Most teenagers and their parents believe that private scholarships are their ticket to underwriting a college education. They also assume that industriousness will win out because they've heard that millions of dollars in scholarships go unclaimed every year. On both counts, however, they are W-R-O-N-G!

Private scholarships are the puniest source of college cash. Federal and state governments and colleges themselves represent more bountiful resources for college-bound students. Only about 7% of college students receive a private scholarship, and the average award is roughly $2,500. They are often only good for one year. So if you work hard to win scholarships to cover your freshman year, you will still have to deal with three years of college costs.

As for the belief that millions of dollars in scholarships go unused each year, here's the actual reality: The only scholarships that typically go unclaimed are so narrowly focused that nobody qualifies. For example, Loyola University in Chicago has a scholarship that covers the tuition of Catholic students whose last name is Zolp. Texas A&M University bestows a full-ride scholarship to students with the last name of Scarpinato.

Hidden Danger

Private scholarships can actually be a financial bust for the students who most need help. Enterprising students who capture private scholarships can end up jeopardizing a portion of their financial aid award. Here's why: federal rules require that a school consider outside scholarship money when calculating its financial aid packages. Let's say, for instance, that a household's expected family contribution (see Chapter 4, "Who Gets Financial Aid") is $15,000, and the cost of the college is $25,000. The school offers a financial aid package of $10,000 to fill the gap. Now let's suppose that the student wins a $2,000 scholarship. The school would reduce its financial aid package by $2,000.

When this occurs, it's better if a college reduces the loan amount rather than a grant that needn't be repaid. Some schools will and some won't. Some colleges will reduce the size of both the grant and the loan. Ask financial aid administrators at the institutions that interest you about their policies regarding private scholarships.

Ironically, private scholarships can be a better alternative for rich students. Why? Wealthy students don't qualify for need-based aid so they are in no danger of losing this money. They do qualify for merit awards, known in the industry as non-need-based aid, but these grants are not impacted by outside private scholarships.

Finding Private Scholarships

If you're interested in hunting for private scholarships, here are some tips to increase your odds:

Reevaluate aiming for top scholarships. The best-known and most lucrative scholarships will be the hardest to win. Mega awards like the Coca-Cola Scholars attract a national audience, so the odds of winning will be miniscule.

Aim lower. It should be easier to win scholarships in your own community and region. Does your workplace offer scholarships to children of employees? Some unions also kick in money for the right student. Service organizations are good places to contact. Also check for scholarships in your high school's counseling department. Visit the resource desk at the local library.

Explore online scholarship tools. Online scholarship locators will simplify your job. Once at the free sites, you can personalize your search by typing in your interests, accomplishments, and other unique aspects about yourself. The database will compare your profile with the requirements of countless scholarships and spit out a list of possibilities.

Here are three prominent scholarships search sites:

- **Fastweb**, www.fastweb.com
- **ScholarPRO**, www.scholarpro.com
- **Scholarships.com**, www.scholarships.com

The most successful treasure hunters will be the ones who approach the scholarship process as a part-time job.

Know who is more likely to win scholarships. Mark Kantrowitz, who is publisher at Fastweb, shares in his slim book *Secrets to Winning a Scholarship* some of the characteristics of teenagers who are more likely to win private scholarships. Here are some of the factors that typically boost an applicant's chances:

- Higher grade point averages
- Higher ACT/SAT scores
- Majoring in engineering or science

- White
- Attending private high school
- Participating in community service

Kantrowitz suggests that students apply to all scholarships for which they are eligible. Who wins is a bit random, even among talented students, so applying to every scholarship that matches your background is the best way to maximize your chances of winning one. After your first half dozen or so applications, students find that they can reuse previous application essays, saving a lot of time.

Beware of scholarship rip-offs. Free college financial seminars can be ripe breeding grounds for rip-off artists. If you are dealing with legitimate professionals, they won't promise that your child will win a scholarship or grant. Be skeptical of any testimonials that you hear from audience members. They could easily be planted in the room to generate sales.

How do you know if you are dealing with a shyster? According to the Federal Trade Commission, here are some of their telltale promises:

- The scholarship is guaranteed or you'll get your money back.
- You can't get this information anywhere else.
- The outfit asks for a credit card or bank account number to hold the scholarship.
- The scholarship will cost money.
- You're a finalist in a contest that you never entered.

Learn more about scholarship scams at the Federal Trade Commission's website at www.ftc.gov/scholarshipscams. To file a complaint with the FTC call (877) FTC-HELP. Other contacts, if you suspect a scam, are the local Better Business Bureau and your state's department of consumer protection.

Action Plan

Unless your child is a stellar standout, focus on regional or local scholarships. Typically these outside scholarships won't be as lucrative as merit awards that schools distribute.

11

Will Saving for College Hurt Your Financial Aid Chances?

Families who save for college are in a much better position than families who do not.

—Mark Kantrowitz, publisher FinAid.org

One night after I had finished a talk at a suburban Philadelphia high school, a parent broached a subject that he didn't want others still lingering in the auditorium to hear.

He asked me if it would be okay to hide money for financial aid purposes. He had received an inheritance, and he was worried that it would hurt his teenager's chances for receiving need-based aid.

I explained to him that hiding money for financial aid purposes is illegal. As it turned out, the amount of money he inherited, about $100,000, would make little impact on his teenager's odds of receiving need-based aid.

While most parents aren't interested in breaking the law to obtain more financial aid, moms and dads are often worried that the money they have saved for college will disqualify them for financial help. If you are stressed about your college accounts—or any other assets—sabotaging your aid chances, relax. Most of the time, parent and child savings are a nonissue in financial aid calculations. In fact, less than 4% of families, who complete financial aid forms, have their financial aid reduced because of the parents' savings.

The Assets That Don't Matter

To appreciate how money in the bank rarely impacts aid awards, you have to understand what counts and what doesn't in federal financial aid calculations. You may be surprised at the assortment of assets that don't count. The federal aid formula doesn't care about home equity nor your qualified retirement accounts such as 401(k) and 403(b) plans and Individual Retirement Accounts. Curiously enough, the formula also doesn't care about assets tied to a family-owned business that employs fewer than 100 employees.

Some private institutions may factor in your retirement accounts when calculating financial aid, but they are rare.

The vast majority of colleges and universities never even know how much an applicant's family has saved up for retirement, which is where the bulk of people's savings reside. The Free Application for Federal Student Aid, which is the form that all families must complete if they want financial aid, doesn't even ask parents or teenagers if they possess qualified retirements accounts.

Parent Assets Enjoy Favorable Treatment

Let's turn to the assets that federal aid methodology does care about. You must divulge if you own property beyond a family residence. You also must share the value of your nonretirement assets. These assets include taxable investment accounts, as well as checking and savings accounts. You also must share the value of your 529 college savings plans and Coverdell Education Savings Accounts, which are considered parent assets.

Colleges do not expect all of a family's assets to be available to pay for college. Parents, after all, have lots of other things that they need to buy, including a new fridge when the old one conks out and a roof when the hailstorm destroys it and braces for the younger kids. Consequently, for financial aid purposes, parent assets are assessed at a maximum of 5.64%. What that means is that for every $10,000 a family has tucked inside a 529 plan, need-based aid would be reduced by $564.

Here's another example: let's say you have $50,000 in a 529 savings account. When you multiply that amount by 5.64%, you'd get $2,820. Consequently, your *expected family contribution*, which is the amount of money a college will expect you to kick in at a minimum for one year of schooling, would increase by $2,820. (See Chapters 4 through 6 for more on EFCs.) The higher the EFC, typically the more money you will be obliged to pay for college.

Parent Asset Allowance

In reality, however, it's unlikely that parental assets would result in any reduction in aid eligibility because families get to shield some of their nonretirement money through something called a federal asset protection allowance.

The asset allowance, which is built into the federal aid formula, generally ranges from $40,000 to $60,000. The exact amount depends on the age of the oldest parent. The older the mother or father is, the greater the allowance. If the oldest parent was 50, for instance, the asset allowance would be $46,600. In contrast, a 45-year-old parent's allowance would be $41,300 while a 60-year-old's would be $61,400. The allowance isn't as large for younger parents because they aren't as close to retirement age.

Let's use the father in Pennsylvania to illustrate why cheating, beyond its illegality, would have been crazy. (Committing fraud on the FAFSA, by the way, can land the filer in prison for up to five years with a maximum fine of $20,000.) Let's assume that the dad is 55 years old, which would give him an allowance of $53,400. Subtracting $53,400 from that $100,000 inheritance would leave him with $46,600, which would be assessed at 5.64%. The $100,000 inheritance would potentially reduce aid by $2,628. If the dad had inherited retirement accounts, the vast majority of schools would not count any portion of the $100,000.

If you'd like to take a look at the latest federal asset protection allowance table, just Google *"EFC formula"* and *"gov."*

Teenager Assets

So far I've focused on parent assets, but teenager assets must also be reported on the FAFSA. It's the question of what assets belong to a teenager versus the parents that often befuddles families. If you hope to qualify for financial aid, it's best to have the college money sitting in parental accounts.

Teenage assets would include whatever cash is in the student's checking or savings account, but that rarely amounts to enough money to shrink an aid package. The big impact asset that a child may own is a custodial UGMA or UTMA, which years ago used to be a popular way for parents to save for college. While it's the parents who routinely stuffed money into these accounts, the cash belongs to the child. The federal formula assesses teenage assets at a higher rate—20%.

Luckily, there is a way to avoid the big financial hit that custodial accounts incur. Parents can move the assets out of the custodial account, pay the resulting taxes, and then transfer the cash to a *custodial* 529 plan. The child still owns the 529, but for financial aid purposes, it's treated as a parent asset just like regular 529 plans.

The Other Financial Aid Application

Up until now, I've focused exclusively on the FAFSA, which is the only aid application that most families need to complete.

About 250 mostly private, selective schools also require an additional aid application called the CSS/Financial Aid PROFILE. The five public institutions that use the PROFILE for undergrads are the University of North Carolina, University of Arizona, University of Michigan, University of Virginia, and College of William and Mary.

The PROFILE's multiplier that is used to assess parent assets can vary between 4% and 6%. The PROFILE assesses student assets at 25%. Schools using the PROFILE often take the value of a home or family-run business into account when determining financial aid packages.

Action Plan

It's always wise to save for college because you will enjoy more options. Worrying about the financial aid impact of your assets is usually pointless.

12

Maximizing Financial Aid

Faced with backbreaking colleges costs, parents desperately try to appear impoverished for financial-aid purposes. But that is trickier than it seems.

—Jonathan Clements, former *Wall Street Journal* columnist

How do you qualify for more financial aid?

That's a preoccupation of many parents. There are ways that families can increase their eligibility for more need-based aid, but frankly these ideas can only impact aid at the margins. Whether a family qualifies for need-based aid most often depends on their income. How much income you earn in a year is the biggest factor.

That said, it's important to understand the basic rules that schools use to determine who qualifies for financial aid. Two families could enjoy the same incomes and net worth and have saved the exact same amount for college, but one could snag a financial award and another could walk away with nothing but loans.

If you're puzzled about how you play the game, here are practical steps you can take to boost your chances of receiving need-based financial aid:

Watch your financial footprints. Many parents assume that colleges aren't going to care about their family finances until their children are seniors in high school. That, however, is a dangerous assumption. You need to be mindful of any financial moves that you make from sophomore year in high school through the senior year.

Schools are going to focus on your family's finances in the so-called base year, which refers to the calendar tax year prior to the year your child starts college. The base year for a child entering college in the fall of 2015, for example, would be 2014.

During this time period, you want to be extremely careful to avoid—if possible—any financial transactions that will jeopardize your chances at aid. Of course, if you've got a zero chance of qualifying for need-based aid, you can ignore all the advice in this chapter.

Your aim should be to minimize the appearance of assets and income in this critical year. There are plenty of legal ways to pull this off. If you have credit card debt or a car loan, for instance, you may want to pay it down earlier than you contemplated. You could also contribute more to a retirement account. By doing these things, you'll have less cash on hand when it's time to complete aid applications. If you expect a year-end bonus, ideally you'll want to get it before the base year starts.

Once you're in that crucial base year, it's best to avoid selling profitable mutual funds, stocks, and other investments. The aid formula counts investment profits as income.

Don't touch retirement accounts. As long as the money stays in a retirement account, the vast majority of schools aren't going to care how much you've saved. You could have $5 million stockpiled in retirement accounts and it wouldn't hurt your chances for financial aid. A few private colleges, however, may factor in your retirement accounts when calculating financial need. Any college or university, however, will take note if you tap into your retirement nest egg. Withdrawals from retirement accounts are considered income, even it is a tax-free return of contributions from a Roth IRA.

Another no-no is converting a traditional Individual Retirement Account into a Roth IRA in the base year. While a Roth conversion can make perfect sense as a retirement strategy, it could be a disaster if you're angling for financial aid. That's because the money that's moved from a traditional IRA into a Roth will be considered income. Financial aid administrators, however, are able to use their professional judgment to disregard the conversion.

Don't let up. Okay, you might be wondering what happens if you do all this for one year? Don't you need to file for financial aid at least three more years? That's true. The financial aid calculations are done annually, but the initial calculation can make the biggest impression.

You would unfortunately face the same challenges every year. Ideally, you'll want to use the strategies to obtain financial aid until roughly the end of your child's junior year. By then you would have submitted your last financial aid application.

Pay attention to where the college money is kept. Unless you know that financial aid is an impossibility, be careful about where you stash the cash. That's because financial aid formulas treat children's assets far more harshly than the money that's in mom and dad's name.

It's easy to argue that treating one pot of money dramatically differently from another just because it's in a different type of account is ridiculous. After all, we're talking about one child's education whether parents saved the money or the child tucked away money from babysitting or cutting the lawn. The system is even more infuriating because the financial aid rules regarding various types of accounts keep evolving. Imagine striking out the last batter in the World Series only to be told that it now requires four strikes to retire the hitter. That's what parents are potentially up against.

So what are the rules? If you're going to qualify for financial aid, it's typically best to have the college money sitting in parental accounts. In the federal formula, the parents' assets will be assessed at no more than 5.64%. In contrast, a child's money will be assessed at 20%. Any cash sitting inside a custodial account belongs to the child. The most common custodial accounts are the Uniform Gifts to Minors Act (UGMA) and Uniform Transfer to Minors Act (UTMA).

Consider moving custodial cash. Luckily, there are ways to legally move cash out of custodial accounts. You don't have to wait until college to spend money in a traditional custodial account. You can dip into a custodial account to pay for summer camp, tutoring, or anything else that doesn't fall into the category of household needs such as the mortgage or food.

Parents can also transfer custodial money into a custodial 529 college plan. Custodial 529 plans are treated as a parental asset if the student is a dependent.

Be an early bird. Imagine billions of dollars of financial aid money sitting in a feed trough and you'll be able to appreciate why it's important to show up for breakfast early.

There are deadlines for state grants, which you don't want to miss. Some states have deadlines at the beginning of March or earlier for their college grant programs. In addition, some states award their grants on a first-come, first-served basis. Apply too late for aid at colleges and universities and the available financial aid revenue might be greatly diminished or gone.

So what's early? You should file the FAFSA as soon after January 1 as possible, which is when the latest form will be available.

You may also have to file the CSS/Financial Aid PROFILE, the financial aid form used by about 250 mostly private schools. The PROFILE is available in October for the following year's freshman class.

To answer many of the questions on both the FAFSA and PROFILE, you'll need to pull numbers off your tax return. That's why it's critical to complete your tax return as soon as possible after January 1.

Of course, tackling taxes that early will seem like an impossible task for many. Self-employed parents can have it even tougher since their tax returns can be more complicated and require gathering many more documents.

Luckily, there is a solution to this problem. You can file an estimated FAFSA and PROFILE and update it later. It's easy to correct the information on an estimated FAFSA by using the federal data retrieval tool. About two weeks after filing your federal income taxes, your tax figures will be available for electronic download into the FAFSA. All families should use this retrieval tool regardless of whether they estimate their taxes.

Pay attention to deadlines. If you miss a school's deadline for financial aid, your aid application may never be reviewed. Overlooking a financial aid deadline can be worse than missing a mortgage payment. Ask schools on your child's list about their financial aid dates.

Avoid financial aid schemes. When seeking outside advice, watch out for piranha. Some insurance agents, in particular, have dived into this niche as a way to sell life insurance and variable annuities to unsuspecting parents. Life insurance is an expensive and unnecessary way to invest for college, as are variable annuities.

Some of these sharks, which are angling for big commissions, encourage parents to transfer their home equity into insurance products so the money will escape the notice of financial aid formulas. What these ethically challenged salesmen don't tell people is that the vast majority of schools don't even examine the value of a home. If someone suggests cashing in your home equity for an annuity or life insurance, run.

Action Plan

To boost your chances of financial aid, you need to start planning well in advance of your child's high school graduation.

13

More Ways to Shrink the Cost of College

The person who does not ask will never get a bargain.

—French Proverb

Need more ideas to clip college costs? Here are a few more:

Lean on your kids. Even if you can afford to underwrite all four (or more) years of your child's college career, don't do it. Your child, despite his or her whining, will greatly benefit from paying at least part of the tab. If teenagers haven't spent time cleaning a deep fat fryer at McDonald's or playing Candyland for the 10th time at a baby-sitting gig, it can be difficult for them to appreciate how hard people have to work for their money.

If they enter college still thinking that money is imbued with magical properties—it just appears when needed—they could ultimately have a much tougher time dealing with the realities of the working world. And before that milestone, they may have more trouble buckling down at school because they don't own a financial stake in their education.

It's important to talk with your child long before freshman year is looming about how much money he must contribute to his college education. You might decide that your child has to pay for certain expenses, such as textbooks and living expenses. Another idea is for him to kick in the equivalent of what he can borrow yearly through the federal Stafford loans, which are designed for students.

Holding a part-time job not only defrays costs, but it can also boost your child's grade point average. Studies show that college students who work part time typically enjoy higher grades than those who don't. Juggling school and work commitments is an excellent skill to develop for a future career.

Leave the car at home. Many colleges would prefer that students, particularly underclassmen, keep their cars at home. You can save a nice chunk of change by dry-docking your kid's car. Obviously, the gas bill disappears and the maintenance costs should shrivel too. What's more, you may be able to freeze the insurance payments until your child returns home.

Even if your child doesn't own a car, you should contact your insurer when she leaves in the fall. Some insurers slash the price of a student's coverage or eliminate the cost entirely until she starts driving again. This can make up for the expense of airfare when attending distant schools.

Don't just look on the coasts. Private East Coast schools are in demand, and they price themselves accordingly. Many of them will soon be charging $60,000 a year. You can often find greater values by looking at wonderful schools in the Midwest and South. Some schools in those regions can cost at least $10,000 less than some comparable institutions on the East Coast.

Become a residential advisor. If your child is responsible and blessed with good social skills, she might want to become a resident assistant. An RA serves as surrogate mother hen to the students in a dormitory. They help settle disputes and make sure students aren't doing dumb things like hauling beer kegs into their dorm rooms. Colleges and universities generally reward their RAs, who typically have to be sophomores or upperclassmen, by eliminating or reducing their room and/or board expenses.

Collect cheap college credits. Taking Advanced Placement or International Baccalaureate courses while in high school can shave a semester or more from an undergraduate career. Another alternative is getting college credits through the College-Level Examination Program (CLEP), which allows students of any age to demonstrate proficiency in college courses. High school students can also obtain college credit by taking community college classes in the summer.

Buy used books. According to one federal study, the cost of textbooks has jumped nearly four times the rate of inflation since 1994.

Expect to be gouged if you wander into your college's bookstore and buy new textbooks. You can save by buying or renting books online.

Apply for free. College expenses start adding up even before you enroll. It can cost $60 to $70 a pop just to apply to colleges. A website called Free College Applications maintains a list of many schools that offer free or reduced price applications. Just Google the name to find it. Low-income students can often obtain fee waivers.

Check for discounts. Ask a school if it grants a discount for a second child who attends, or for recommending the school to a friend who enrolls.

Check out work colleges. Students enrolled at working colleges pay no tuition or significantly reduced fees. Everyone holds a job at these colleges, which integrate work with academics. While there were hundreds of these colleges in the mid-nineteenth century, today only seven schools meet the federal definition of a working college. Students work on campus farms, repair computers, work at daycare centers for the community, and operate dining halls. The vast majority of students work at least 140 hours per semester.

These three working schools do not charge tuition:

- **Berea College, Berea, Kentucky,** which an abolitionist started in the mid 1800s as the South's first interracial and coeducational college, reaches out to promising students, who couldn't go to college without a helping hand. The free offer attracts so many applicants that the acceptance rate is 12%.
- **College of the Ozarks, Point Lookout, Missouri,** calls itself Hard Work U. Just like Berea, the school's popularity has shrunk its acceptance rate to 10%.
- **Alice Lloyd College, Pippa Passes, Kentucky.** The school's tuition is waived for students who live in a 108-county area of Appalachia that crosses into five states.

Here are the remaining working colleges:

- Blackburn College, Carlinville, Illinois
- Ecclesia College, Springdale, Arkansas

- Sterling College, Craftsbury Common, Vermont
- Warren Wilson College, Asheville, North Carolina

In addition, Knoxville College in Knoxville, Tennessee, which was involved in a working program until the late 1920s, is actively seeking to revive it. Berry College in Mount Berry, Georgia, shares many of the traits of a working college.

To learn more about working colleges, visit the website of the Work Colleges Consortium (www.workcolleges.org).

Action Plan

Students should pay a portion of their college costs. Having a part-time job can actually improve a student's grades.

14

Appealing the Verdict

What the (financial aid) formula tries to do is put everyone in square boxes, pin them to a grid, and say: This is how much money you need to go to college. So what the appeals process does is it allows the families to explain why they're not square.

—Maureen McRae, Occidental College's director of financial aid

If you were a college financial aid administrator, would you give a teenager whose parents had racked up big gambling losses a bigger aid package?

That's the dilemma that faced the financial aid appeals committee at Occidental College in Los Angeles, which reviewed an appeal from a teenager whose parents are addicted gamblers. Her mom and dad's gambling winnings, the young woman wrote in a letter, inflated the family's income. Their gambling losses, however, dwarfed their earnings.

This was one of the cases that Occidental's appeals committee reviewed that *The Chronicle of Higher Education* captured in an article that provided an inside look at how aid appeals are handled.

During the deliberation over this gambling case, Maureen McRae, the director of financial aid, made this observation: "If this was 'Dad lost his job,' or had one-time lottery winnings, or went on Jeopardy!, we would be looking at this differently. Or if this was a coke addiction and all the money went up his nose, would we be looking at it differently than a gambling addiction?"

Someone on the committee suggested that they wait to see if the accepted student showed up at the school's open house to measure her commitment or invite the young woman, who doesn't live far away, to the school for a conversation.

The committee members, who believed gambling is an addiction, ultimately decided that they wanted the girl to attend Occidental. The staffers were impressed by her initiative to write a well-crafted letter that detailed the financial predicament her family faced. Her college essay also illustrated these qualities. The committee decided to ask the family for its latest two tax returns and see what happens.

I am sharing this story because it illustrates that financial aid appeals can work in the right circumstances. Many families assume that the aid packages that they receive at private and public colleges and universities are final, but this isn't always true.

What the case of the gamblers' daughter strongly suggests is that families who appeal have a better chance of succeeding if their teenagers are strong students.

When a student is barely accepted into a college, it's often less likely that the family will capture more aid regardless of how poignant his plea is. Financial aid is finite, and colleges will reserve any extra for those whom they covet. This is going to be particularly true at private schools.

Wealthy students can also appeal their merit scholarships, but this will be a tougher case to make. During the Occidental deliberations, for instance, committee members were unimpressed by an appeal from a rich student who had received merit scholarships from other colleges but not Occidental. Like many schools, Occidental gives merit scholarships based on the strength of the individual students. The admission director was quoted as saying the family "should have been ashamed" because they clearly could afford the school without a price cut.

What To Do When Appealing an Award

If you decide to appeal a financial aid package, here are eight things to keep in mind:

1. **Pinpoint a school's appeal process.** Look on the school's website to see if the appeal procedure is posted. Sometimes families must complete an online appeal form. When sending emails or letters to the aid office, make sure you find out the right person to address correspondence.

2. **Contact the school.** It's best to call the school and explain that you have questions about the aid package. If you don't live nearby, ask for a phone appointment with an aid officer. If you hear nothing, follow up with a call or email.

3. **Have a conversation.** Some aid experts suggest that parents and/or teenagers provide a specific dollar amount that they need. Others, including Myra Baas Smith, the College Board's executive director of financial aid services and former director of student financial services at Yale University and Smith College, recommends against that approach. Smith once told me that if families approach the discussion as a "conversation, it's much easier for the aid person to get a better sense of your family and what your real needs are."

4. **Skip the tears.** Financial aid officers hate to see parents cry or shout or in anyway show the kind of emotions that would make them want to flee the room or hang up the phone. They hate histrionics. Instead, talk dispassionately when you request that the school reexamine its aid package and also provide documentation that supports your need for more assistance.

5. **Don't overlook extenuating circumstances.** You should alert a school's financial aid officer to circumstances that might boost your package. This is important because the federal financial aid form doesn't provide space to mention extenuating circumstances. These can include parents taking care of an aging parent, high medical bills, or a one-time bonus that inflated the family's income

Also, after a family completes the financial aid applications, plenty can change. If a parent loses a job, dies, becomes disabled, or the family experiences some other financial hardship, let the college know.

6. **Try leverage.** Let's suppose your child received solid aid packages from other schools, but the college where he is aching to attend wasn't nearly as generous. If this happens, contact the college with the smaller package and explain that your child received higher offers elsewhere. Don't gloat about the better awards or act indignant that the school wasn't as generous from the outset. You should resist using the word "negotiate." Just explain that your child would really love to attend the school, but the financial strain would be far less elsewhere.

   For this strategy to have a chance of working, however, the schools should be competing for the same universe of kids. An aid administrator at Carnegie Mellon University, for instance, isn't going to be impressed if your child earned a merit scholarship from a nonselective school in rural Oklahoma. Carnegie Mellon University is known for its policy of considering other offers. On its website it says: "We are open to negotiating financial awards to compete with other institutions."

   The daughter of a friend of mine tried this during the last admission season and was successful. Her No. 1 choice was California Lutheran University, but this school gave her the smallest yearly aid package ($9,100). She received better offers from other schools including Linfield College ($13,770), Dominican University ($11,150), and Pacific Lutheran University ($10,678). My friend contacted Cal Lutheran and requested a review of her daughter's package. After supplying the school with the other offers, Cal Lutheran boosted the package an additional $3,500 a year to $12,600.

7. **Reexamine your paperwork.** When completing financial aid applications, mistakes happen. In fact, by one estimate, 90% of families make a mistake when they fill out the FAFSA. Slipped decimal points, transcribed figures, and other mishaps occur

frequently. Some parents leave a question blank instead of inserting a zero. The wrong Social Security number is typed in or parents supply the monthly income instead of yearly. If you're disappointed or surprised by your child's aid package or lack of one, reexamine your figures.

8. **Realize that colleges can make errors.** It's not just parents who goof up. Errors can occur when institutions are processing thousands of applications on tight deadlines. So if an aid verdict seems wrong, it may be. That's what happened to one student, who received significant financial aid packages from Dartmouth College and Tufts University but got zilch from Yale University. The family submitted copies of the aid offers from the other schools and ultimately they were rewarded for taking that extra step. Yale had overlooked something in its financial assessment and corrected the oversight by producing its own award package.

Action Plan

Don't assume that a college's first financial aid offer is the final one. In some circumstances, appealing an award can pay off.

15

Getting Grandma to Help

Grandparents and 529s were made for each other.

—Joseph Hurley, CPA, Savingforcollege.com

When grandparents want to help with college costs, this should be the No. 1 rule that they follow: First, do no harm.

To illustrate what can go wrong if you ignore this admonition, I'm sharing the story of a middle-class family in Southern California that received a large financial gift from a wealthy grandparent. The grandfather gave each of the three children a significant amount of money that he wanted them to eventually use to purchase homes for themselves.

There was, however, an unintended consequence of the grandfather's largesse. His gifts ensured that his grandchildren would not qualify for financial aid. One of the children had been interested in attending a private college, but if he had done so, he would have had to use that future house money to pay the tab. Rather than do that, he is attending a state school with lower costs, and his family is covering the bill.

The teenagers in this family would have enjoyed more college options if the grandfather had waited a few years to give his grandchildren the money.

Obviously grandparents don't want their generosity to backfire, which is why parents and grandparents need to understand the safe ways to help out. Here's what grandma and grandpa need to know before they try to assist with college costs.

Understand if a gift will have a negative impact. If a family is affluent and will not qualify for any need-based financial aid, there is no reason to stress about the consequences of a grandparent's gift. The handling of a grandparent's gift will be a potential issue only if a family has a chance of qualifying for need-based aid.

Understand the rules for 529 college savings plans. Many generous grandparents invest in 529 college savings plans for their grandkids. These 529 plans allow the account holders to shelter college money from federal and often state taxes. Account holders can withdraw money in these college savings accounts without triggering taxes.

Many families assume that it's safe for grandparents to sink unlimited amounts of money into 529 plans because nobody is going to ask about grandma's money on financial aid forms. That's not, however, entirely correct.

It is true that the Free Application for Federal Student Aid or FAFSA, which is the most common financial aid form, doesn't care if grandparents possess college accounts. There isn't any question on the form that asks about this. A grandparent could stash a lot of money inside a 529 plan, and it won't hurt the grandchild's aid chances as long as this cash stays inside the account.

When a grandparent, however, withdraws 529 cash to help defray college costs, the financial aid formula will take note. That's because the parents will have to report the grandparent's contribution as untaxed income on the FAFSA, as well as the CSS/Financial Aid PROFILE. The PROFILE is a financial aid form used by mostly private colleges and universities.

The impact of untaxed income can be significant if the withdrawal is large enough. That's because the untaxed income is considered to be the child's. A teen's income is taxed at up to 50% for financial aid purposes. Consequently, this income could end up reducing aid eligibility by as much as half of the cash withdrawn from the college account.

Reevaluate paying the tab directly. Some grandparents assume that the best way to help their grandkids is to send a check directly to the college. But here's where the generosity can backfire: Many universities shrink the size of a child's financial aid package by the amount of the grandparent's check. If a school has awarded the student $15,000 and grandma mailed the university a check for $15,000, the financial aid could vanish.

Before writing a check, a parent or grandparent should contact the school and ask whether the payment would jeopardize the child's financial aid award. This obviously won't be an issue if the school is not providing any financial assistance to the child.

Wait awhile. There is a way for grandparents to provide money for college without jeopardizing financial aid. Grandparents can give the money to the child after the last financial aid forms are submitted in the spring of his or her junior year in college. This usually is the preferable option.

Give the money to the parents. Yet another option is to give the cash to the parents, who unlike their child, would not be required to mention the gift on the FAFSA. They would, however, have to report the money as an asset. While parent assets are assessed less severely than child assets, an extra $100,000 in parent assets, for example, could reduce aid eligibility by as much as $5,640.

Evaluate a custodial account. These accounts are a bad idea if a grandchild will eventually qualify for financial aid. The common custodial accounts are the Uniform Transfers to Minors Act (UTMA) and the Uniform Gifts to Minors Act (UGMA), which grandparents can open at many financial institutions. See Chapter 12, "Maximizing Financial Aid," for more on these accounts.

Action Plan

Grandparents can be a godsend when helping with college costs, but make sure they don't sabotage their grandchildren's chances for financial aid.

Part II

Increasing Your Admission Chances

16

Boosting Your Chances

How admissions offices contrive to meet all these institu-
tional needs—how they manage to enroll pre-meds, painters,
children of alumni ("legacies"), soccer players, Exeter grads,
and African-Americans in roughly the same proportions,
year after year—while maintaining (or improving) the col-
lege's median S.A.T. score is a good story, and it's made bet-
ter by the understandable reluctance of most colleges to speak
frankly about the process.

—Louis Menand, *The New Yorker* magazine

When a Certified Public Accountant from upstate New York con-templated how he was going to afford his son's college, he knew he didn't want to pay the sticker price.

The son was a good student, though he wasn't anywhere near the top of his class. The CPA figured that if he proceeded strategically, his son could win a price break.

As the father and son started searching for colleges, they made sure the list contained good academic fits that were located in dif-ferent regions. He ultimately applied to five schools—Lynchburg College in Lynchburg, Virginia; Seattle (Washington) University; Hartwick College in Oneonta, New York; West Virginia University; and the State University of New York at Albany.

The teenager won merit scholarships at all the private schools that he applied to, including Hartwick College where he enrolled. "If we had not done any planning at all," the CPA recalled, "we would have had a big college bill."

The son and his dad did several things right in their pursuit to find schools at a more affordable price. First, they didn't overreach. The teenager applied only to schools that represented solid academic fits, which are more likely to award merit money. The family also looked beyond their geographic region, which can also make the applicant look more attractive. While the young man obviously couldn't control his gender, being a guy could have also helped his chances at the liberal arts colleges, where coeds routinely outnumber the men on campus.

Just as this family in New York state did, parents and teenagers should approach the college admission process more strategically to make this major expense less costly. In the next 11 chapters, you will learn how to do just that.

Action Plan

Teenagers are more likely to win greater awards from colleges if they apply strategically to colleges.

17

Finding the Right Match

It used to be that you could try for that reach school and if you got in, you didn't have to worry because everybody who got in, who needed money, got money. Today, however, as colleges are asked to fund more and more of their own operations with less and less assistance from the government, foundations, and families, they are increasingly reluctant to part with their money to enroll students who don't raise their academic profile.

—*The Real Deal on Financial Aid*, Muhlenberg College Office of Admissions

A teenager from Seattle—let's call him Matt—had spent his high school years at the top of his class. He had experienced one academic success after another, which made him assume that getting into an Ivy League university should be doable if he applied to enough of them.

The teenager completed applications for several Ivy League schools, including Harvard, Dartmouth, and Brown. He was surprised and hurt when he received rejections from all of them. (I'm mystified why teenagers are surprised when Ivy League schools reject them!) Matt did get into his three non-Ivy picks: the University of California, Berkeley, UCLA, and Chapman University in Orange County, California.

Matt discovered, however, that the UC schools were prohibitively expensive for a nonresident (see Chapter 8, "The Allure of Out-of-State Public Universities"), which provided him with only one school left standing—Chapman. I'm not in a position to say whether Chapman was a suitable pick for the brilliant teenager, but what was unfortunate was that he had boxed himself into a corner and was left with just one realistic choice.

Selecting Schools Strategically

There is a lesson to be learned from Matt's travails, and here it is: Teenagers should develop lists of schools that represent good academic and financial fits. Teenagers who do this increase their chances of ending up with a fistful of acceptance letters from schools that are willing to cut the price for them.

So how do students pull this off? When looking for matches, teenagers should typically aim for colleges where they would be in the top 25% to 33% of the applicants. This is especially important if they require financial aid or merit scholarships to attend a school.

Why is being in the top third or so of applicants important? Because schools don't possess unlimited resources to offer scholarships to everyone, so they strategically ration their grants. The students whom an institution is nuts about are the ones more likely to be rewarded, and that's true for students of all income levels. Schools are typically willing to cut the price for top applicants, but they may have no desire or ability to make their degrees financially doable for teenagers whose academic profiles aren't as impressive.

Schools are much more likely to bestow favored students with preferential financial aid packages. The best packages include primarily grants (scholarships) and sometimes not even a single loan. Which teenagers enjoy VIP treatment depends on the overall academic profile of the institution's student body. Here's an example: A teen has a 3.8 GPA and 1300 SAT (on a 1600 scale), and is applying to a school where the students in the 75th percentile of its most recent freshman class earned a 3.5 GPA and a 1240 SAT. At this school, the teenager would be a highly desirable applicant.

The Hazard of Reach Schools

In contrast, schools often exhibit little enthusiasm in offering financial carrots to teenagers whose academic profiles aren't as impressive. Teenagers who fall into this category include those who apply to so-called *reach schools*. A reach school is one where the applicant has little chance of getting accepted. Here's a reach-school example: A teenager who has earned a 2.9 GPA and an ACT score of 19 applies to a college where the most recent freshman class had an average GPA of 3.6 and an ACT score of 25, while the top 25% of its first-year students had an average GPA of 3.8 and a 29 ACT.

It's possible that the teenager with the 2.9 GPA beats the odds and gets admitted to this college. The student, however, would more likely receive a financial aid package stuffed with loans. If the child came from a wealthy family, it is doubtful that he would receive any scholarship.

Getting into a school where a student barely qualifies can wreak financial havoc on families that require help paying for college. High school counselors, however, routinely urge students to include reach schools on their lists, apparently unaware of the financial hazards of doing so.

Unfortunately, college admission reps often don't level with teenagers about their chances for admission or receiving financial assistance. You rarely hear a rep tell a teenager something like this: "Hey, our school would be a real reach for you, and you might want to keep looking." Admission reps are more likely to function as cheerleaders who urge students to apply and who brag about their wide range of scholarships. I understand why they do this. Colleges are businesses, and, as such, they are eager to attract as many applicants as possible.

So how does Matt's story fit in here? Matt, after all, possessed the same sort of grades and test scores that successful applicants to Ivy League schools earned. The eight Ivy League institutions and perhaps three-dozen or so other elite schools represent a special case because the vast majority of applicants are rejected even though they enjoy impeccable credentials. These institutions should be considered reach schools for nearly all applicants. With rejection rates of 85% to 90% or higher, these schools can't be considered a match for anyone unless a parent is arguably a highly regarded celebrity, a billionaire, or a U.S. president. If you aren't in that group, you're facing a rejection rate that's even worse than the published one.

Matt squandered his chances of developing a solid list of schools by throwing the dice on too many Ivy League institutions. He would have fared better if he had focused on academically rigorous schools that aren't so impossibly hard to get into. I'm not suggesting that students should avoid applying to schools that seem unattainable, but don't waste the majority of your applications on long-shot schools.

Reach School Exceptions

Some students can safely apply to a reach school. The most notable are rich students. If the parents make enough money to pay the full price, then applying to a reach school couldn't hurt. They shouldn't, however, apply to too many of these schools, or they could face the same dilemma as Matt. As you'll learn in Chapter 23, "Why Being Rich Helps," being wealthy can boost the admission fortunes of average students.

There is also no financial risk for a student to apply to schools that offer excellent aid packages to all qualified students. The institutions that fall into that category are elite institutions with large endowments that include the Ivy League schools. At these universities, the last student in the door still qualifies for the same generous financial aid treatment as everybody else who requires assistance. Once again, however, students should only apply to these schools sparingly and only if their academic profiles are stellar.

Weighing the Odds

If your child isn't in the top third of an applicant pool, this doesn't mean that she will be shut out of merit awards. At some schools, particularly lesser-known private ones, nearly everyone receives some type of grant. An easy way to pinpoint the percentage of students who receive institutional grants is to head to the federal College Navigator website that's linked to a huge database of information about the nation's colleges and universities. You can find College Navigator by Googling it.

Once on the site, type in the name of the school and then click on its financial aid link and look at the *institutional grants or scholarship* line. You will see the percentage of freshmen who receive grants from the school, as well as what the average grant is. For instance, at Hendrix College, a highly respected liberal arts college in Arkansas, 100% of students received a grant, and the average was worth $20,006.

You can also use the federal College Navigator website to find a variety of statistics for individual schools in such categories as net prices, majors, graduation rates, and freshman retention.

Action Plan

Students who require financial aid are generally better off applying to schools where they are in the top 25% to 33% of the applicants academically.

Students can compare their GPAs and standardized test scores with the typical scores of students attending a particular school by looking at its profile on the College Navigator, as well as collegiate guides such as those published by *Fiske* and the *Princeton Review*.

18

Ditching the Test

With colleges and universities engaged in intense competition to recruit ever more talented and diverse students, test-optional policies become alluring.

—Jonathan P. Epstein, higher-education consultant

How do teenagers increase their chances of getting accepted to colleges, much less winning attractive awards if they bomb on the SAT and/or ACT?

That's a question that haunts parents of bright, hardworking teenagers who don't test well. Some poor test takers are slow readers. Others freeze when they are stuck in a room with a test booklet and sharpened No. 2 pencils. Some kids ace the reading section and stink on the math questions. Still others are handicapped by their high schools, which don't prepare them as well as schools with very high academic standards and a raft of Advanced Placement class offerings.

In the face of continual criticism about the test's relevance and fairness, a critical mass of schools offer a way to neutralize poor test scores. Roughly 850 colleges and universities have made the SAT and ACT optional in their admission process. These schools represent one-third of all accredited bachelor-degree granting institutions.

The number of test-optional schools is somewhat misleading because many of these institutions have admission requirements that aren't difficult. Some of these institutions, for instance, maintain open-enrollment admission policies, meaning just about anybody is accepted whether or not they submit scores.

Excellent Test-Optional Colleges

There are, however, stellar colleges and universities in the test-optional lineup, particularly among liberal arts colleges. The test-optional policy is perfect for liberal arts colleges because these institutions enjoy the luxuries of evaluating applicants holistically and spending more time with each application. Lawrence University, a liberal arts college in Wisconsin, for instance, has roughly 2,700 applications to review versus more than 21,000 that the admission staff at George Washington University must process.

More than a third of the schools that belong on *US News & World Report*'s list of the top 100 liberal arts schools have instituted a test-optional policy. Some of these institutions include Bates College, Mount Holyoke College, Pitzer College, Franklin and Marshall College, College of the Holy Cross, Furman University, Lawrence University, Bard College, Gettysburg College, and Dickinson College.

Test-optional adoption has been a much tougher sell at selective universities where there's far more of an admission emphasis on test scores, grade point averages, and class rank. Schools that receive tens of thousands of applications don't have the luxury of getting acquainted with each teenager. A notable exception to this rule is Wake Forest University, which revamped its admission procedure to embrace the test-optional policy. Wake Forest administrators, by the way, say the test-optional policy has allowed the school to attract a much stronger freshman class. Other schools in the national university category that have gone test optional include American University, DePaul University, New School, Worcester Polytechnic Institute, University of Arizona, and George Mason University.

The universities, which *US News* characterizes as regional institutions, are more likely to embrace test-optional policies. They include schools such as Providence College, Loyola University in Maryland, Seton Hall University, Rollins College, Bryant University, Baldwin-Wallace College, and Whitworth University.

What Is Test Optional?

Test-optional policies vary by school. For the test phobic, Sarah Lawrence College instituted the ideal policy. The liberal arts college is technically not a test-optional school because it won't accept test scores from *any* of its applicants. There's no point in submitting standardized test scores to this New York school because it won't accept them.

Not all colleges are as generous with the test-challenged as it might seem. Some schools, for example, may only waive the test for students who meet a minimum grade point average or who have reached a certain class rank. Certain schools make teenagers without test scores submit samples of graded work from high school.

Some schools are "test-flexible," which means a student can choose—in lieu of the SAT or ACT—other scores to submit such as from Advanced Placement and International Baccalaureate exams. Some test-flexible schools require the scores of SAT subject tests. The test-flexible liberal arts colleges are Middlebury, Hamilton, Bryn Mawr, Colby, Colorado, and Trinity colleges.

Many schools, by the way, do not require ACT/SAT scores from non-traditional age applicants. Transfer students, as well as those with documented learning disabilities, may also be able to avoid submitting scores.

What the Supporters Say

I agree with those who believe that test-optional policies make the college admissions process fairer. It opens up more schools to minority applicants, as well as those from less affluent households and talented teenagers who do poorly on standardized tests. (Of course, a school could be more inclusive simply by giving less weight to the tests for all or selected applicants.) It also helps level the playing field among those who can afford expensive SAT tutoring and those whose only preparation is a good night's sleep.

One of the leading SAT critics is the National Center for Fair & Open Testing (FairTest), which is a nonprofit dedicated to fighting standardized testing. It argues that SAT scores are an inadequate predictor of how a student will fare at college and whether they will graduate. Despite significant differences in instructional quality at high schools, studies have shown that the best predictor of college success is a teenager's high school grade point average.

After living with its test-optional policy for more than two decades, Bates College in Maine accumulated extensive data that shows that its students' performance remains strong. After gathering five years of data of its experience, Hamilton College concluded that the students who don't submit their test scores do slightly better academically than their peers.

You can obtain the list of test-optional schools by visiting the website of FairTest (www.fairtest.org). The schools on the list, according to the organization, "de-emphasize" the use of standardized testing. To survive the cut, schools must make admission decisions about a substantial number of applicants without relying on the ACT or SAT.

The Cynical Reasons Behind Test-Optional Policies

Skeptics argue that plenty of the schools have ditched the SAT for cynical reasons. If an institution, for instance, eliminates the SAT requirement, it often sees an immediate 10% to 20% bump in the number of applications it receives. When word gets out about the change in policy, teens with lackluster test scores conclude that they now may qualify for a school that they once considered unattainable.

Schools are delighted when they receive more applications because it allows them to appear more exclusive. How does that happen? When a school is deluged with applications, it can reject far more teenagers. As perverse as this may seem to many anxious families, *US News* favors schools that reject the greatest percentage of applicants.

If a school becomes test optional, the institution's average test scores for its incoming freshman class also often improve. After all, teenagers with lackluster scores are the ones not likely to submit them. Consequently, published scores at test-optional schools can be artificially high.

Switching to a test-optional policy can raise the average SAT scores by 20 to 30 points. And guess what? The *US News & World Report* formula will reward schools that can brag about higher SAT scores since they don't care how these figures are generated. The head of *US News'* college rankings, however, has said that going test optional has not altered any school's ranking. Higher scores, however, do make a school appear to attract higher-caliber students.

Unfortunately, very few test-optional institutions do the right thing and add the ignored scores into their annual published test averages. I know of only four schools that go to the trouble of obtaining the scores from nonsubmitters after the admission process is finished and use them in the official averages. The four schools, which should be commended, are DePaul University, Muhlenberg College, Providence College, and Wake Forest University.

If you are eager to sit on your test scores, here is something to keep in mind: Rich students who hope to capture merit awards could be disappointed if they fail to share their scores with certain schools. When writing an article for *The New York Times* on SAT-optional issues in 2009, I contacted 37 top liberal arts colleges with test-optional policies and eight told me that they required SAT or ACT scores for one or more of their merit awards. The schools said failure to submit scores would not impact need-based financial aid.

Test-Optional Naysayer

In an op-ed piece in *The New York Times*, Colin S. Diver, president of Reed College in Portland, Oregon, provided this withering take on the test-optional trend: "I sometimes think I should write a handbook for college admission officials titled, 'How to Play the *US News & World Report* Ranking Game, and Win!' I would devote the first chapter to a tactic called 'SAT optional.'" Diver called the move toward SAT optional admissions a "disheartening" trend. "In the rush to climb the pecking order, educational institutions are adopting practices, and rationalization for those practices, unworthy of the intellectual rigor they seek to instill in their students."

Action Plan

Regardless of what others think or why schools have adopted test-optional policies, applying to test-optional schools can be a great way to eliminate lackluster scores as an admission hurdle.

19

Showing a College Some Love

For colleges that try to bring 100% science to the admissions process, it (stealth applications) is very disruptive. It adds more art to the equation.

—Jeff Rickey, dean of admissions and financial aid at Earlham College

All colleges and universities like to be loved, but some want to be courted more than others.

To increase your chances of getting into a college, and possibly receiving more money, you should determine whether a school wants to be shown a little love.

Before you can do that, however, you need to understand a term called *demonstrated interest*. This is higher-ed jargon that refers to a teenager's active interest in a school. A teenager who has visited a campus, for example, has shown a demonstrated interest. Requesting marketing material via the college's website is another way to demonstrate interest.

While it might conjure up visions of Big Brother, many institutions track contacts with high school students. There is a practical explanation for keeping tabs. Being able to tell what students have taken the time to pick up the phone, send an email, or attend an open-house weekend can help schools differentiate between students who may be marginally interested in them and those who will end up as serious candidates. Accept too many ho-hum applicants and a school's yield—the number of accepted freshmen who end up enrolling—can plunge. And that can wreak havoc with a school's revenue.

Don't Be a Stealth Applicant

High school students, however, are increasingly skipping the courtship step. A growing number are applying without ever checking in with a school beforehand. The Internet has made it possible for students to research schools without this step. Colleges have nicknamed these students *stealth applicants*.

Failing to contact a school before you apply is generally unadvisable. At a minimum, it will take you 60 seconds to complete an online form asking for a school's marketing material, so why not do it? You should absolutely make the effort if you are applying to a school that wants to know you exist before you submit your application. In its annual survey of schools, the National Association for College Admission Counseling concluded that more than one out of five institutions consider an applicant's demonstrated interest of *considerable importance* in its admission decisions.

The Naval, Air Force, and U.S. Military academies are among the schools that consider demonstrated interest important. That's understandable because students are going to be signing up for more than just four years of schooling. Private colleges, which evaluate applicants holistically, also fall into this category. In contrast, state universities generally aren't going to give students an admissions boost for visiting a campus or requesting marketing materials. Private universities vary on the importance they place on students getting in touch before they apply.

Checking a School's Common Data Set

So how do you know if a school values personal contact? An easy way to find out is to look at an institution's *Common Data Set*, which is an annual document that many colleges and universities complete and make available on their websites. The best way to find a school's Common Data Set is to Google the term and the name of the school. In section *C. First-Time, First-Year (Freshmen) Admission* of each school's Common Data Set, the institution ranks the importance of 19 admission factors, including an applicant's level of interest.

Each school ranks the 19 admission factors in one of these four categories:

- Very important
- Important
- Considered
- Not considered

When researching a school, you should also look at how a school feels about all 19 factors. Here they are:

Academic factors

- Rigor of secondary school record
- Class rank
- Academic GPA
- Standardized test scores
- Application essay
- Recommendation(s)

Nonacademic factors

- Interview
- Extracurricular activities
- Talent/ability
- Character/personal qualities
- First generation
- Alumni/ae relation
- Geographical residence
- State residency
- Religious affiliation/commitment
- Racial/ethnic status
- Volunteer work
- Work experience
- Level of interest

You can also find the admission factors for individual schools by looking at their profiles on the websites of COLLEGEdata and the College Board's BigFuture website. To find the factors at BigFuture (http://bigfuture.org), type in the name of the school in the search box on the home page. Once the school's profile appears, click on its Applying hyperlink. You'll find the admission factors under the What's Important? tab.

Showing Your Interest in a School

You can express interest in a school through a variety of ways, including these:

- Request materials via the college's website.
- Stop by a college's booth at a college fair or when a rep visits your high school.
- Visit a college's virtual open house at CollegeWeekLive.com.
- Chat live with a student online via the school's admission website.
- Visit a school's Facebook pages and use a school's other social media outlets such as Foursquare and YouTube.
- Follow the school on Twitter.
- Arrange a college tour.

At institutions that value inquiries from potential students, teenagers should look on a school's website and find out whether there is a regional admission rep for their state or area. Students should contact the appropriate admission officer by email and explain that they are interested in the school. Teenagers should do this only after they've done research on a college and can ask some intelligent questions.

Teenagers should also ask whether a rep will be in their area so they can meet. Many schools send admission officers on the road every year to meet prospective students. Fall is the biggest time for this travel.

Action Plan

Expressing interest in a school is one of the easiest ways to get an admissions boost.

20

When Talent Is the Hook

I have no special talent. I am only passionately curious.

—Albert Einstein

Are you a singer or a dancer? How about a dedicated volunteer? Or perhaps you're a committed environmentalist, an artist, or a promising entrepreneur? Maybe you're a future scientist who conducts experiments in your basement.

Colleges and universities adore students with talents. Teenagers who can demonstrate particular talents, whether it's being fluent in two or three languages or starting a thriving business in high school, can help their admission chances.

Colleges are so eager to attract students with a wide range of talents that many of them offer these applicants an opportunity to win in-house scholarships. I'm not referring to merit scholarships that teenagers are automatically considered for when they apply to a school. Those scholarships represent the bulk of the awards. I'm referring to lesser-known scholarship opportunities that require teenagers to complete separate applications. In some cases, such as musical, dance, and theatrical scholarships, an audition could be required.

Talent Scholarships Can Be Overlooked

Institutional talent scholarships often don't have nearly as much competition as private scholarships, which are overrated as a source of college cash. (See Chapter 10, "Capturing Private Scholarships.") These talent scholarships can be quite lucrative.

My son Ben, for instance, applied for a science scholarship at Lake Forest College in Illinois that is given to students interested in the sciences. In his scholarship application, Ben had to include a list of math and science courses he had taken in high school and his grades, mention any notable science programs or research projects he had completed, along with science honors. Applicants for the scholarship were also encouraged to visit the campus and talk with a science professor. Ben was stoked when he ended up getting the maximum award of $8,000 a year, but he ended up attending a different liberal arts college.

My daughter Caitlin also applied for talent scholarships at the school that she ended up attending. She was a finalist for Juniata College's full-ride leadership scholarship (she didn't get it), but she did land the language scholarship for Spanish majors. The school underwrote her experience in southern Mexico one summer and kicked in extra money when she spent a year abroad at the University of Barcelona.

How do you find these extra scholarships? You should check a school's website, and you can also contact the admission office.

You should also head over to MeritAid.com, which provides an exhaustive directory of scholarships offered by individual schools. The availability of scholarships varies dramatically. On the site, for instance, Auburn University and University of Texas, Austin, listed 78 and 166 different scholarships, respectively. In contrast, no talent scholarships were listed for Harvard University, which only provides need-based financial aid.

Action Plan

Before applying to a school, see whether it offers talent scholarships that you might be qualified to win.

21

The Realities of Athletic Scholarships

*Coaches and college admissions share the important inter-
est of needing to make their school attractive to high-caliber
applicants. And because so many otherwise qualified applicants also are interested in athletics, admission officers make
sure that information about the college's sports teams is pre-
sented in the best possible light.*

—Mitchell L. Stevens, author of *Creating a Class:
College Admissions and the Education of Elites*

Do you secretly hope that your son or daughter will win an athletic scholarship?

Don't be shy about admitting it. Lots of parents harbor that wish.
The hope that children will kick, throw, or catch a ball good enough
to underwrite a college education can start before boys or girls have
even memorized their multiplication tables.

My sister, for instance, believes that her daughter Kate, who is a
forward for a top club soccer team in the San Francisco Bay area, has
a chance at a soccer scholarship. Kate, by the way, is just 11 years old.

The chances are miniscule, however, that Kate or any other child
will someday win an athletic scholarship. About 2% of high school
seniors win sports scholarships every year at NCAA schools. The average scholarship, by the way, is less than $11,000.

Being an athlete, however, can boost a teenager's admission chances because all schools, regardless of whether they offer scholarships, desire strong sports programs. Your child doesn't have to be a superstar athlete to increase his or her chances of admission. And your child doesn't need to capture a sports scholarship to ultimately make your college tab more affordable.

In reality, athletic scholarships are often not as generous as regular financial aid or merit scholarships that jocks can earn for their academics and other talents. Striking it big with an athletic scholarship, however, resonates with parents whether their children are still in grade school or well into their high school years.

If sports scholarships sound appealing, here is something to keep in mind: Families often end up shopping for athletic scholarships rather than for schools that represent good academic fits. If you are a gifted athlete or the parent of one, I'd recommend that you first identify schools that would be a match academically and then inquire about the sports. Getting a college education is infinitely more important than playing a sport. And remember, the money you receive for academic accomplishments is often more than a sports scholarship.

Athleticism Won't Make Up for Poor Grades

What's tragic about the focus on sports scholarships is that it encourages students to spend more time on their sport than their grades. Kris Hinz, an independent college counselor, once shared with me her experience with high school athletes that nicely sums up the problem. Here is her observation:

> In my practice, parents often apologize about their kid's grades, then quickly say, "But he's a great athlete and we're hoping that can be his ace in the hole." They are hoping that his athletic prowess will get him accepted and get him money! A tall order! They are usually wrong on both counts. And the worst part is, all the time that has been devoted to sports has siphoned off time that could have been spent studying to earn a strong GPA.

Different Types of Sports Scholarships

When parents dream of sports scholarships, they are typically hoping for full-ride scholarships. There are, however, precious few of them. There are only six sports among schools participating in the National Collegiate Athletic Association where athletes have a good chance of receiving a full-ride award, and they are all within the Division I schools, which tend to offer the bigger sports programs or who aspire to have a national reputation. These are men's football and basketball, as well as women's basketball, tennis, gymnastics, and volleyball. (There are more women's teams on this list in an attempt to even out the large number of men's football scholarships.)

All six of theses sports offer what are called *head count* scholarships. An athlete who captures a Division I scholarship in these sports receives a full ride.

In Division I men's basketball, for instance, a school can offer no more than 13 scholarships. Thirteen student-athletes will capture a full-ride, and the other players are out of luck—they won't receive any athletic money. That's the rule whether you are a basketball powerhouse like Duke and Kansas or a below-the-radar school like Nicholls State and Western Illinois universities.

The NCAA considers all other collegiate athletic programs *equivalency* sports. Under this system, the NCAA dictates the maximum number of scholarships allowed per sport, but full-rides aren't required. Unlike in the head count sports, coaches in the equivalency sports can divide up these scholarships to attract as many promising players as possible. Slicing and dicing scholarships can lead to some pretty small awards.

In Division I men's soccer and swimming/diving, for instance, there are a maximum of 9.9 equivalency scholarships for each sport. Division I women's field hockey and lacrosse each have 12 equivalency scholarships. To attract more students, a coach with 10 scholarships might divide them up so that two-dozen students or more receive something. A top prospect, for example, might receive close to a full-ride, but that would leave less money for the coach to entice other recruits to the team. It's important to know that the vast majority of Division I sports teams do not offer the maximum amount of scholarships permitted because they can't afford it.

Division II schools, which tend to be regionally known universities, have fewer scholarships to offer. For instance, in Division I, a maximum of 85 football scholarships are available versus a ceiling of 36 scholarships for Division II schools.

The Odds of a Getting an Athletic Scholarship

Several years ago, *The New York Times* conducted research to determine what the value of the typical scholarships in each sport was, as well as how many college students received one. It was an eye opener for me, and I've mentioned it to many parents with athletic teenagers. Just Google the name of the article—"Expectations Lose to Reality of Sports Scholarships"—and you'll find the story and an accompanying chart that lists the number of scholarships and average amount by sport. The statistics are sobering.

While the figures are a few years old—I tried and failed to obtain more current ones from the NCAA—I seriously doubt today's numbers would be much different.

The most popular sport for teenage boys is football. When the *NY Times* was doing its research, more than one million boys played on high school teams, and yet there were only 19,549 Division I and II football scholarships divided among 28,299 athletes. The average football scholarship was worth $12,980. The most popular sport for teenage girls was track and field. More than 600,000 girls competed in high school, but there were only 4,506 scholarships. These track scholarships were split among 9,888 athletes. The average scholarship was $8,105.

The chart also dispels the lie that the odds of getting an athletic scholarship are much greater with less popular sports such as lacrosse or field hockey. The only sport I could find where the odds of getting a scholarship appeared excellent was women's rowing. About 2,360 girls rowed on high school teams, and there were 958 rowing scholarships, but they were divided among 2,295 athletes. The average rowing scholarship, after being divided, was $9,723.

Is Beating the Odds a Good Thing?

Let's say your child is a tremendous athlete who beats the odds and wins a large athletic scholarship. Is this something you should celebrate? Maybe, maybe not. Here's why I'm waffling: Schools can essentially treat scholarship recipients as employees.

If you're on a Division I team, you could find that your No. 1 job is to hit home runs, break cross-country records, and score touchdowns. Acing your classes and getting on the honor roll aren't in your job description.

As a Division I athlete, your choice of majors could be limited. Want to be a premed or an engineering major? It's probably not going to happen. Your schedule just won't permit time for science labs or brain-bruising courses that require a lot of homework. A Calculus III professor probably isn't going to like it if you have to skip a couple of days of class each week because you are traveling with the team.

USA Today did a blockbuster study a few years ago that aimed at seeing whether athletes involved in five prominent sports at Division I schools were clustered in certain majors. They discovered that there were indeed high rates of clustering. For instance, 118 of the 142 Division I schools in the investigation had at least one team in which at least 25% of the juniors and seniors majored in the same thing. For instance, seven of the 19 players on Stanford's baseball team majored in sociology.

Sports As a Time Hog

Another potential concern is the hours spent with the coach. The NCAA released a student-athlete satisfaction study in 2011 that included just how many hours students have been devoting to their sports. Here is the average number of hours per week that men and women in Division I spent on their sports. The NCAA only released the hours for the following sports:

Men's Sports	Hours
Baseball	42.1
Basketball	39.2
Football (FBS)	43.3
Football (FCS)	41.6
Other sports	32.0
Women	
Basketball	37.6 hours
Other sports	33.3 hours

An Alternative to NCAA Scholarships

The NCAA only allows Division I and II institutions to award scholarships, but it would be a mistake to think that you can leverage your athletic talent only at schools with sports money. Division III institutions represent another promising opportunity. Division III schools are 80% private and 20% public and include such prominent institutions as the University of Chicago, Tufts University, Amherst College, Williams College, California Institute of Technology, and Washington University in St. Louis.

The NCAA prohibits Division III schools from awarding any athletic money, but they are still keenly interested in their sports programs. All schools are eager for their sports teams to thrive, and a talented goalie, linebacker, or sprinter can enjoy an admission advantage at these Division III schools. The Ivy League schools, while in Division I, also don't award any sports scholarships, but it's been estimated that recruited athletes at these schools enjoy a 40% greater chance of admission.

At Division III schools, there is generally a much greater emphasis on academics, and students don't have to worry about losing their financial support if they stop playing their sport or end up as a benchwarmer. That's because Division III athletes receive need-based financial aid or merit awards that aren't tied to their sports performance. That's a much better arrangement for athletes.

One final way to find money for athleticism is to look at schools participating in the National Association of Intercollegiate Athletics (NAIA), which operates in the shadows of the NCAA. The majority of schools in this association are sectarian schools with small endowments.

Getting Discovered

Do families eager to locate scholarships need to hire a recruiter? I once directed that question to Karen Weaver, the director of athletics at a Penn State satellite campus, who has coached field hockey at four schools, including Williams College, Purdue, and Ohio State. Weaver, who coached one field hockey national championship team, was adamant that recruiters are a waste of time and money.

Coaches typically think that recruiters are pests, says Weaver, who is also a CBS sports commentator. "Coaches really don't want recruiters getting in the middle," she insisted. I also talked with a former women's soccer coach at Tulane and Georgetown universities who concurred.

As a practical matter, recruiters can't possibly know the athletic needs of sports programs across the country even if they suggest otherwise. They are more likely to steer you to programs they know, which won't necessarily represent the best academic fits.

While you don't need a recruiter, you do need to be proactive. Only superstar athletes can count on being discovered. The vast majority of athletes will have to work at it and let coaches know you exist.

I once helped my niece, who is a talented golfer, reach out to golf coaches at Division II schools in the Midwest. Molly crafted a short letter that mentioned some salient statistics about her golf game and attached a golf resume, and within a few hours, all the coaches had emailed her back. She never would have heard from any of them if she hadn't started the conversation.

After pinpointing promising schools, introduce yourself through email. It's a good idea to send the coach a sports resume and to periodically update him or her with emails. Let the coach know, for instance, about your athletic accomplishments and when you will be competing in tournaments. You can send a DVD—or preferably—send a link to a video you've uploaded to YouTube. The video does not need to be more than five to seven minutes long, and it does not have to be professionally shot.

Action Plan

The odds of receiving a sports scholarship are daunting, but being an athlete can give you an admission boost at many schools.

If you want to pursue a sports scholarship, you can't wait to be discovered. You have to contact coaches on your own.

22

The Geographic Hook

Many excellent colleges have trouble enrolling more than a dozen students from states more than 300 to 400 miles away, and will take notice if you're from outside their traditional range.

—Howard and Matthew Greene, independent college consultants

The dean of undergraduate admissions and financial aid at the University of Rochester decided last summer to analyze what admission factors had influenced his school's scholarship decisions.

Among his discoveries was this: Freshmen living outside New York state received an extra $2,000-a-year scholarship. Jonathan Burdick, the admission director, didn't check, but he suspects that the farther the freshmen lived from New York state, the richer the award. During a conversation I had with Burdick, he told me that he was particularly thrilled with the university's three freshmen from New Mexico.

Why is the University of Rochester, where 47% of freshmen hail from outside New York state, eager to reward teenagers from other time zones? This private university values geographic diversity. And so do many, many other schools.

When I attended the welcome weekend for my son and his fellow freshmen at Beloit College, one of the administrators speaking to the families mentioned that there were typically two (or maybe three) states where the Wisconsin liberal arts college routinely fails to attract students. The speaker then proudly announced that the school had a freshman representing South Carolina, one of those hard-to-get states. The administrator called the student to the stage and gave him a Beloit t-shirt while everyone clapped.

Growing Interest in Students from Elsewhere

Private colleges and universities have traditionally coveted students who hail from somewhere else, and as you'll learn, teenage applicants can certainly take advantage of this soft spot for geographic diversity in both gaining admission to a school and possibly fattening their aid offers. More recently, state universities have also been aggressively courting nonresidents in what *The Chronicle of Higher Education* has called "an all-out war for out-of-state students." (See Chapter 8, "The Allure of Out-of-State Public Universities.")

Schools desire students from distant states for a host of reasons. For starters, it can make an institution a richer place to attend when the student body comes from different regions. At Beloit, where 79% of students aren't from Wisconsin, my son has friends from places as diverse as Chicago, Illinois; Littleton, Colorado; Portland, Oregon; Brooklyn, New York; Minneapolis, Minnesota; and Chapel Hill, North Carolina. Ben's best college friend hails from Spearfish, South Dakota, where the family is practically living off the grid.

Colleges that do attract outsiders enjoy bragging about their diversity. Some schools have imposed a map of the United States on their website and share how many students from each state attend their school. Schools routinely highlight students from distant places in their marketing. My daughter, who grew up in Southern California and attended Juniata College in central Pennsylvania, was the only freshman featured in the school's varsity soccer video. She proudly declared to any prospective students watching that she was from "sunny San Diego." Two years later, she was one of the featured students in a guide sent to prospective students. Clearly the message of highlighting students from far away is this: If these kids can schlep 2,000 or 3,000 miles to attend this school, it must be pretty awesome.

Schools are also aggressively attracting students from distant states where the numbers of high school students are declining. The numbers are slipping in such states as Michigan, Ohio, Illinois, all the New England states, New York, and Pennsylvania, as well as Louisiana, Alabama, and Mississippi in the South. The recruiting effort by North Dakota state universities to attract nonresidents has been so aggressive that it prompted a lengthy story in the *Wall Street Journal*. (See Chapter 9, "Looking Across State Lines for a Bargain.")

California is a hot spot for recruiters from private and state institutions. Droves of college representatives from as far away as South Carolina, New Jersey, and Rhode Island have established beachheads there. The message to abandon California for college is resonating with a growing number of California teenagers.

A Geographic Advantage

Some schools value geographic diversity so highly that it can provide students with a powerful hook when applying. In some cases, a student won't have to be as accomplished to gain admission and/or receive an attractive financial aid package or merit award. If an admission committee at an Ohio college, for instance, is deciding who gets a scholarship between two equally talented candidates, who do you think it would be more inclined to award it to—yet another kid who lives in the Cleveland suburbs or someone who resides in Fort Worth or Kansas City?

A weak candidate isn't going to suddenly become marketable because he's willing to hop on a plane to attend college, but a good prospect can become a stronger one by using the geographic hook.

Staying Close to Home

Ironically, most teenagers don't take advantage of this hook. A college counselor at a private boys' high school in St. Louis once mentioned to me that families that he works with aren't interested in their children attending distant schools. He suggested that this was just a peculiarity of Missourians, but I assured him that the feeling was widespread. Families in just about every state in the country, except those in New England where the states are clustered, seem content to have their children attend college in their own states.

Most students attend college within a two-hour drive from their home. According to an annual UCLA survey of freshmen, the vast majority of students never look beyond the public universities in their own states, and 55% don't wander more than 100 miles from home. Only 14% of first-year students attend schools more than 500 miles away from their parents.

These are the states where the greatest percentage of students stays within their borders to attend college:

Texas: 93%

Alaska: 91.5%

California: 91%

Michigan: 90%

New Jersey: 90%

Georgia: 85%

There are certainly legitimate reasons why students would want to remain close to home. Some students don't possess the maturity, but plenty do. I once talked with the former vice president of enrollment at Dickinson College in Pennsylvania, and he noted that the students who attended his liberal arts college from distant states were typically the most mature.

Many families are understandably intimidated by the prices of out-of-state schools. Grants from these schools can make the cost similar to in-state public universities or even cheaper for some applicants. In addition, the extra transportation costs of attending these schools can be negated if a student leaves a car behind. Insurers will often slash the price of a family's auto insurance if a student doesn't drive while in college.

Students who are contemplating attending a far-off institution should make sure it's not a *suitcase school*. If most of the students live close to their homes, they will be more tempted to head home for the weekend leaving the campus feeling deserted. One way to check for this is to head to the College Board's BigFuture website (http://bigfuture.org) and type in the name of a school in the search box. Once on the school's profile page, click on the Campus Life tab to obtain what percentage of students are in-state versus out-of-state.

Action Plan

Applying to schools outside students' own state or region can increase their desirability and their merit awards.

23

Why Being Rich Helps

It sounds immoral to replace really talented low-income kids with less talented richer kids, but unless you're a Williams or an Amherst, the alternative is the quality of the education declines for everyone.

—Morton Owen Schapiro, president of Williams College

Back in 2009, Reed College, a prestigious liberal arts college in Portland, Oregon, was grappling with a sticky issue that ultimately landed it on the front page of *The New York Times*.

Reed College, like some other elite colleges and universities, admirably aimed to accept students strictly on merit. Reed's admission officers reviewed the applications of teenagers without taking into consideration whether they could afford the expensive school.

The college's goal was to assemble the best freshman class possible without worrying about whether the ideal class happened to contain a significant number of students from modest means who required substantial financial aid. Only the wealthiest schools can pull off this sort of need-blind policy, and it turns out, Reed wasn't in that league.

The liberal arts college discovered it had a problem when the admission office's list of accepted applicants contained an excess of students who required financial help. Aggravating matters, too many returning students needed additional financial aid due to the recession. The school increased its financial aid budget by nearly 8% and offered aid to 14% more applicants than the previous year, but it was not enough. Before the notifications were dispatched, Reed's financial aid director told the admission office that it had to remove more than 100 needy students and replace them with wealthy teenagers whose parents could cover the entire tab.

It's unlikely that anybody outside of Reed would have known about the good fortune of the 100-plus wealthy teenagers who bumped stronger applicants. The controversial move, however, was shared with the readers of *The New York Times* because one of its reporters had been allowed to sit in on candid budget discussions. Talk about a public relations nightmare. When the story hit, more than 300 readers posted comments on the newspaper's website, and most of them, let's just say, were unsympathetic to Reed.

A Common Advantage

What got lost in the telling of this story, however, is this: What Reed did is commonplace. During admission deliberations, plenty of rich students benefit on the backs of low- and middle-income teenagers. Schools need the revenue that wealthy students generate to keep their enterprises humming.

Institutions obviously aren't going to talk candidly about this phenomenon because who needs the negative publicity?

I am sharing this story because I think it's important for parents and students of any income to appreciate that rich students can and do receive preferential treatment. Very few schools, as mentioned earlier, can assemble a class without taking the financial wherewithal of at least some of its students into consideration.

More common is an industry practice called *need aware* or *need sensitive*. At schools with these policies, schools do examine the finances of families. The majority of students, however, are selected regardless of their financial neediness. Using this approach, a school will accept most of its freshman class without any regard to its financial bottom line. For the last 10%, 20%, or 30% or so of slots, however, a school will examine the financial ability of applicants, which will favor affluent students. With this admission approach, the students who are borderline applicants AND financially needy are the ones mostly likely to be rejected.

So what happens if your family isn't rich? The best way to avoid experiencing the same fate as the rejected Reed students is to be the best student you can possibly be and then aim for schools that represent great academic matches. (See Chapter 17, "Finding the Right Match.") The more impressive your academic profile is, the more options you will enjoy. Colleges love students of any income who are talented.

Action Plan

If your parents are wealthy, you may enjoy a competitive advantage in getting into college.

If your parents are low- or middle-income, it's important to select schools that represent solid academic matches because those institutions are more likely to accept you and provide greater financial aid.

24

The Legacy Hook

Most Americans are firmly committed to notions of meritoc-
racy—the conviction that opportunity and mobility should
be based on ability and performance and not on the circum-
stances of one's birth, including the social position of one's
parents.

—Thomas J. Espenshade, a Princeton professor of sociology
and the author of *No Longer Separate, Not Yet Equal: Race*
and Class in Elite College Admission and Campus Life

If your mom or dad graduated from an elite school like Georgetown, Columbia, Harvard, Cornell, Johns Hopkins, or Stanford,
congratulations; you possess a secret admission weapon—your birth
certificate.

At many of the nation's wealthiest and most prestigious schools,
whom your mother and father are matters a great deal. If your dad
graduated from Princeton, for instance, you enjoy a better chance of
sliding past the school's admission bouncers. In some cases, you can
even scoot closer to the front of the line if a sibling or a grandparent
attended a school.

Virtually all elite liberal arts colleges and three quarters of selective research universities practice legacy favoritism, according to
Richard D. Kahlenberg, a senior fellow at the Century Foundation
and the author of an excellent and exhaustive book on the topic, *Affir-*
mative Action for the Rich: Legacy Preferences in College Admissions.

While there is a perception that legacy admissions are a custom
confined to private institutions founded back when gentlemen were
still wearing powdered wigs, it's not true. Plenty of public universities

also maintain legacy policies including the College of William and Mary, Auburn, Indiana, Purdue, and Penn State, as well as the Universities of Florida, Michigan, Minnesota, North Carolina, Connecticut, Delaware, Virginia, Maryland, and Wisconsin.

Legacy Admission Advantage

What kind of admission advantage do legacies enjoy? Children of alumni often make up 10% to 25% of the student body at elite schools. In contrast, at the California Institute of Technology, a highly prestigious school that doesn't believe in legacy favoritism, only 1.5% of students are children of alumni.

Admission deans, who are loathe to talk about this issue, like to suggest that the favoritism is reserved for times when a tiebreaker is necessary. For example, an admission committee that is looking at two equally qualified candidates will give the nod to the kid whose mom is an alum. Research, however, suggests the admission advantage can be far more significant.

Research from Thomas Espenshade, a Princeton sociologist, concluded that legacy applicants on average received the equivalent of an additional 160 points on the SAT's combined math/reading test that has a maximum of 1600 points. That's quite a boost!

Supporters argue that a legacy advantage is a necessary evil for a school's bottom line. Parents, particularly those with deep pockets, are going to be more generous if they think it will help their own children get into their alma mater. This conventional wisdom, however, is erroneous. Studies have suggested that there is no causal relationship between a school's legacy policies and total alumni giving at prestigious universities.

Legacy preferences are a uniquely American phenomenon, which got its start after World War I under dubious circumstances. Elite private colleges and universities were concerned about the growing numbers of immigrant students, and especially Jewish ones, who were outshining the traditional students of wealthy families through academic admission criteria. This spurred some schools to impose Jewish quotas, but when they became too loathsome to defend, institutions switched to less tangible admission factors such as character, geographic diversity, and legacy status.

Action Plan

In the admission race toward the most elite schools, legacy applicants enjoy a head start. If you're a legacy, thank your parent(s) for this advantage.

25

Playing the Gender Card

We have told today's young women that the world is their oyster; the problem is, so many of them believed us that the standards for admission to today's most selective colleges are stiffer for women than men. How's that for an unintended consequence of the women's liberation movement?

—Jennifer Delahunty Britz, dean of admissions and financial aid at Kenyon College

My daughter was a junior in high school when I read an op-ed piece in *The New York Times* that was written by a mother whose daughter was upset that she had been waitlisted at one of the five colleges on her list.

The essay grabbed my attention because the mother was hardly the average parent who rails against the inanity of the college admissions process. The author happened to be the dean of admissions and financial aid at Kenyon College, a prestigious liberal arts college in Gambier, Ohio.

What made me panic was the mournful acknowledgment by Jennifer Delahunty Britz that admissions officers at Kenyon and other schools are rejecting wonderfully accomplished teenage girls simply because of their gender. And the reason? Frankly, there are just too many of them. Females now represent 57% of the nation's college undergraduates, and the presence of men on college campuses is expected to continue dropping.

Gender Tipping Point

College administrators are leery of letting the gender divide grow too wide on their campuses. Some believe that the tipping point is reached when women make up 60% or more of the student body. When that happens, female applicants will sometimes look for campuses with a closer ratio of men and women. And teenage boys will cross these male-lite schools off their list because they don't want to be too outnumbered. Or at least that is the fear.

These lopsided percentages have led to a practice that can incense the parents of teenage girls. At some institutions, admissions offices are trying to bring the numbers back to equilibrium by giving boys a break. (This is chiefly a private college phenomenon.) At the same time that schools are rejecting qualified girls, they are embracing male candidates who can thank their Y-chromosomes, in part, for their admission letters.

Here are a couple of examples of schools that have been accepting more men than women. At Kenyon College, the acceptance rate for young women was recently 30.9% versus 37.3% for men. Swarthmore College, an elite liberal arts college in Pennsylvania, recently accepted 17.7% of its male applicants and 13.2% of the women who applied.

In 2009, the U.S. Commission on Civil Rights launched an investigation into whether certain liberal arts colleges were rejecting too many female applicants. The probe was controversial, and it was shut down without releasing any conclusions in 2011.

Advantage for Teenage Girls

Teenage boys don't enjoy all the advantages. Young women can capture a competitive advantage if they apply to schools where men predominate. These, of course, are usually the schools best known for their engineering programs and other technical degrees.

In its latest admission figures, the Massachusetts Institute of Technology, for instance, accepted 15.5% of women, but just 7.5% of men. At the California Institute of Technology, the acceptance rates were 9.1% for male applicants and 23.1% for women. The most astounding gender advantage that I found was at Harvey Mudd College, a prestigious engineering/liberal arts college outside Los Angeles. Forty eight percent of women were accepted, but just 17% of male applicants.

Using Gender as a Hook

What should you do, now that you know the role that gender plays in some admission decisions? Look at gender disparities not only when contemplating your child's chances of getting into a particular school but also in terms of his or her chances of receiving financial awards. A school that is eagerly seeking more boys or girls could be more generous to those who check the right gender box on their application.

It should be easy to find out what a school's admission track record is for each sex. Just look at a school's annual Common Data Set, which is a compilation of a variety of institutional statistics that includes how many applicants of each gender apply to the school and how many are accepted. You will find gender statistics in section C of the yearly document. Many colleges and universities post their Common Data Set on their websites. A quick way to find the document is to Google the name of the school and the term *"Common Data Set."* You can also hunt for the data in the Institutional Research section of a school's website.

Action Plan

Teenage girls can enjoy greater admission success by applying to engineering schools and other institutions that attract more teenage boys.

Young men can sometimes benefit by applying to schools where the majority of students are women.

26

Diversity Blueprint

At a time when more and more low-income and minority students are preparing for college, it is disturbing that many of our most prestigious colleges and universities are turning away from them.

—Kati Haycock, president of The Education Trust

When my son was in high school, the teenagers in his carpool got free college advice from me. The advice wasn't always solicited, but the four kids did listen politely.

Madison was one of those teenagers who sat in the backseat of my old Volvo station wagon while we navigated rush hour traffic on one of San Diego's congested freeways.

Madison had an above average grade point average, but his SAT scores were just average. Madison, who is a musician, happened to be one of the most interesting and mature teenagers I had ever met. He was thoughtful, articulate, and engaging. And he struck me as a resilient kid who could leave San Diego for college and not crumble. I thought there were some private schools, which evaluate applicants holistically, that would love to have a kid like Madison.

One of Madison's other hooks was something he had no control over. Madison's dad was black, and his mom was Hispanic. I saw his racial background as a favorable admission hook that can help some students who have a lot on the ball. Madison, however, told me that playing a racial card didn't seem fair. Nonsense, I responded. Lots of students use hooks to get into college, and those who enjoy the biggest admission advantage are rich students. (See Chapter 23, "Why Being Rich Helps.")

State universities dominated Madison's original list of schools. He was particularly interested in San Diego State, a couple of miles from his house, and San Francisco State. While the tuition at these schools is relatively low, the room and board is high, and the odds of graduating in four years are grim. San Francisco State's four-year grad rate is less than 12%.

I encouraged Madison to add some liberal arts colleges to his list, and one that I suggested was Beloit College in Wisconsin. An admission rep from the liberal arts college was going to be visiting Madison's high school, and I told Madison to make sure he scheduled an interview, which he did. A few weeks after Madison applied to Beloit, his mom ran over to my car as I pulled into the carpool meeting spot near Trader Joe's. She blurted out that Madison had won a $100,000 diversity scholarship from Beloit.

Beloit ended up flying Madison to accepted student day, and he fell in love with the school after spending a weekend on the campus and meeting students and faculty. He's a creative writing and Japanese major, who joined a fraternity, became a campus disc jockey, and spent time in Japan.

I am sharing Madison's story, because it helps illustrates this little-known reality: It's possible for a minority student with few resources to end up attending an excellent school for a fraction of the sticker price. And yes, it can help to be a smart student who also happens to be black, Hispanic, Native American Indian, and sometimes Asian American.

Reasons for Diverse Campuses

There are a host of reasons why some private and public colleges and universities maintain policies that favor minority candidates. Helping students who might not go to college otherwise is one compelling reason.

Diversity is another motivator. At many private schools, the student bodies are predominantly affluent and white. It makes for a richer environment if there is a mix of students from different racial and ethnic backgrounds. Here's an additional explanation: After reviewing recent research about student learning, two prominent academics who wrote the influential book, *How College Affects Students: A Third Decade of Research*, concluded that good teaching and exposure to students from diverse backgrounds are two of the strongest predictors of whether college freshmen will return and also improve their critical thinking skills.

In some states, public universities can favor minority students, but in others, most notably in California, affirmative action is forbidden. By the time you read this chapter, the U.S. Supreme Court may have ruled on an affirmative action challenge brought by a young white woman, who was rejected from the University of Texas at Austin.

Any favoritism that a school shows toward minority applicants isn't something that you will discover on a college's website or in marketing material. To find out, you have to ask. That's what I've done when talking with admission officers at college fairs and other venues. I'll inquire whether minority teens receive a break on test scores and grade point averages. I've had good luck getting candid answers from them.

Looking Beyond the Obvious

Talented minority students frequently overlook schools that they assume cost too much or are too exclusive. *The Journal of Blacks in Higher Education*, however, has collected data over the years that documents that many prestigious liberal arts schools warmly embrace black applicants. The journal compiled the following acceptance list that suggests that cracking some elite colleges isn't as hard for a smart African American. I don't have comparable figures for other minorities, but you can assume that the right candidates can also enjoy a break.

	Overall Acceptance Rate	Blacks Acceptance Rate
Amherst College	15.3%	31.1%
Swarthmore College	16.1%	30.3%
Vassar College	23.6%	31.5%
Oberlin College	33.2%	40.5%

	Overall Acceptance Rate	Blacks Acceptance Rate
Pomona College	14.7%	28.3%
Haverford College	26.0%	30.0%
Bowdoin College	19.7%	40.4%
Wellesley College	33.3%	41.4%
Colby College	34.2%	45.3%
Bates College	31.5%	38.1%
Grinnell College	38.4%	45.1%
Trinity College	43.2%	52.8%
Middlebury College	19.2%	41.2%

Minority Test Advantage

Thomas J. Espenshade, a Princeton economist, wrote a highly lauded book, *No Longer Separate, Not Yet Equal: Race and Class in Elite College Admission and Campus Life*, that looked at the admission practices of ten of the nation's highly selective schools and concluded that some minority groups, as well as students from certain income classes, enjoyed advantages.

When examining SAT and ACT scores at the unnamed schools, the researchers discovered that black students enjoyed the most striking test advantages after controlling for such factors as gender, grades, and type of high school attended.

In Table 25.1, you'll see that the academics used white and middle-class students' average test scores as the norm. Compared to white students, a black test taker enjoyed a 310-point SAT advantage on a 1600 scale and a 3.8-point advantage on the ACT, which has a maximum score of 36. A black student who scored a 1100 on the SAT, for example, would have the same chance of admission at the elite schools as a white student who scores a 1410.

The advantage for Hispanic students—.3 points on the ACT and 130 points on the SAT—was far smaller. Meanwhile, Asian students were penalized. On the SAT, Asian Americans had to have scores 140 points higher to enjoy the same chance of admission. (See the next chapter for more on Asian-American students.) You can find a nice synopsis of Espenshade's research at the website of Inside Higher Ed, a trade publication, by Googling the name of the publication and "The Power of Race."

Table 25.1 Advantages by Race and Class on the SAT and ACT at Selective Colleges, Fall 1997

Group	Public Institutions (on ACT scale of 36)	Private Institutions (on SAT scale of 1,600)
Race		
White	--	--
Black	+3.8	+310
Hispanic	+0.3	+130
Asian	-3.4	-140
Class		
Lower	-0.1	+130
Working	+0.0	+70
Middle	--	--
Upper-Middle	+0.3	+50
Upper	+0.4	-30

While talented minority students do enjoy advantages at some schools, many rarely even know about these opportunities and neither do their high school counselors. Here's what's ironic about affirmative action policies. Some schools that have them aren't putting much effort into finding the disadvantaged kids. How good are these practices if students aren't even aware that they exist? In Chapter 3, "The Colleges with the Best Financial Aid," I mention how some of the wealthiest schools in the country, including Washington University in St. Louis, University of Notre Dame, and some Ivy League schools have low percentages of poor students, which would encompass many first-generation college goers.

At this point, you might assume that the minority applicants who are enjoying admission advantages are all underprivileged kids, but that's not true. A potentially controversial aspect of the drive to increase diversity on campuses is that schools can seem more interested in attracting minority applicants who are comfortable financially and who have parents who are college graduates.

Where Minority Students Attend College

Many minority students limit their college choices to the most obvious picks. For instance, according to Excelencia in Education, which is a nonprofit policy group, about half of Hispanic undergraduate students attend just 6% of the nation's colleges and universities.

These schools are considered Hispanic-Serving Institutions (HSI) because 25% or more of the undergraduate student body are Hispanics. Places with a significant number of these institutions include campuses connected to the University of Puerto Rico, California State University, City University of New York, Los Angeles Community College District, and the University of Texas. The heavily Hispanic institutions tend to be relatively inexpensive, maintain lower admission standards, and serve students who live nearby. Many of these institutions, however, have poor graduation rates.

Foundations and other nonprofits are devoting a tremendous amount of energy and money to develop ways to ensure that more minority students go to college and succeed. Unfortunately, schools have mixed track records on graduating minority students. Nationwide, 60% of white students earn a bachelor's degree within six years, while 49% of Hispanics and 40% of African Americans do.

An Education Trust report illustrated that some schools with similar demographics can boast similar grad rates for all students, while others are dismal. One school that the report cited was Wayne State University in Detroit, where only one in ten African Americans graduated within six years. The grad rate for white students was more than four times higher.

Minority students can check the grad-rate statistics of four-year schools by visiting the website of College Results Online (www.collegeresults.org), which is a service of The Education Trust. You can find the overall grad rates for a school, as well as those broken down by gender and for under-represented minorities.

Paying for College

Ambitious minority students might assume that their best way to pay for college is to apply for private scholarships, but often they can be harder to get. White students win the majority of them, according to Mark Kantrowitz, the publisher of FastWeb, the most popular scholarship search engine. What's more, winning a private scholarship can ultimately reduce a low-income student's financial aid package. (See Chapter 10, "Capturing Private Scholarships.")

A better game plan for minority teenagers can be to focus on being the best student possible. The better a student's academic record, the more likely she will get into more selective colleges and universities that provide greater financial aid. The money that a college or university can provide—particularly private institutions—can far exceed government help.

Minority Resources

A helpful resource for first-generation, low-income, and minority students is the Center for Student Opportunity, which you can find at www.csopportunity.org.

The Center for Student Opportunity provides an online clearinghouse of college programs and admissions information for students, parents, and counselors for minority and underserved students. They also facilitate pro-bono work offered by professional college counselors who want to help low-income schools and community-based organizations.

Another resource is Pathways to College Network, which is sponsored by The Institute for Higher Education Policy (www.pathways tocollege.net). On the site, you can find an online directory of resources for middle- and high-school students to prepare for college.

Action Plan

Smart minority students can enjoy an advantage at some selective colleges, but the majority attend public institutions where the graduation rates are underwhelming.

27

The Asian Student Dilemma

Chinese parents can order their kids to get straight As.
Western parents can only ask their kids to try their best.

—Amy Chua, Yale Law professor and author of *Battle Hymn of the Tiger Mother*

If you are an Asian-American teenager, have you been tempted to hide your heritage when applying to colleges?

This isn't an odd question. Asian Americans who have set their sights on elite universities are worried that getting into a school like Harvard or Dartmouth will be harder if their last name is Li, Wong, Kim, or Tanaka. Many Asian Americans are not revealing their ethnicity on their applications or are identifying themselves as multiracial. When one parent is of a different ethnicity, students are using that one.

Asian-American teenagers, along with their parents, complain that they are being stereotyped as academic robots whose only interest is doing whatever it takes to get into Ivy League schools and other uber prestigious schools.

Amy Chua, a Yale law professor who wrote the controversial book *Battle Hymn of the Tiger Mother*, inadvertently became a lightning rod and poster mom for this stereotype when her prescription for raising Asian-American children was published. With an Ivy League education a goal, Chua wouldn't let her two daughters watch television or play computer games, choose their own extracurricular activities, attend sleepovers, or play any instrument other than the piano or violin. Chua viewed any grade less than an A as unacceptable, and the daughters were expected to be the No. 1 student in every subject except PE and drama. (Months after the book created a firestorm, Chua's oldest daughter was accepted into Harvard and Yale.)

So do Asian Americans have a legitimate complaint? Research, as well as circumstantial evidence, suggests that they do experience a harder time getting into the most elite schools. Before I share research that has generated considerable consternation among Asian families, let's take a look at the percentage of Asian students at the eight Ivy League institutions:

Percentage of Asians in Ivy League Freshman Classes

Brown University: 12%

Dartmouth College: 14%

Cornell: 15%

Harvard: 15%

Yale: 16%

University of Pennsylvania: 17%

Princeton University: 18%

Columbia University: 19%

The percentages of Asians at these elite schools, while higher than the Asian population in the nation (6%), represent a fairly narrow band. It's interesting to compare the Ivy League percentages to those at campuses in the University of California system, where race, by state law, cannot be used in admission decisions. At these state universities, there is a heavy reliance on grades in college-prep courses and class rank in admission decisions. In a largely numbers-driven admission process, the percentages of Asians at UC schools are dramatically higher.

Percentage of Asians at University of California Campuses

University of California, San Diego: 50%

University of California, Irvine: 49%

University of California, Berkeley: 40%

University of California, Santa Barbara: 36%

University of California, Los Angeles: 34%

It's understandable if Asians looking at the Ivy League statistics would conclude that the playing field isn't fair. And that's certainly the argument that they could make after reading the results of research conducted by Thomas J. Espenshade, a Princeton sociologist, that was compiled in the book *No Longer Separate, Not Yet Equal: Race and Class in Elite College Admission and Campus Life*. Espenshade and another researcher examined federal data and analyzed institutional records and student surveys at eight elite, but unnamed, public and private institutions. One of their focuses was on whether race hurt or helped applicants at these prestigious schools.

After controlling for such factors as gender and high school grades, the research showed that Asians did have to earn higher SAT and ACT scores to compete for admission. (See the previous chapter.) An Asian student required an extra 140 points on the SAT to have the same chance of admission as a white student.

A major reason why it is hard for bright Asian Americans to get into these elite schools is because so many of them are applying to the same two dozen or so elite research universities. There is a perception, particularly among Asian immigrant families, that the best way to succeed professionally is to attend a school like Princeton or Yale. This perception is unfortunate to say the least.

There's Hope!

While Asian-American teenagers and their parents will find this research discouraging, it's important to appreciate that the Asian disadvantage is nonexistent at most schools. The vast majority of colleges and universities are eager to have more Asian students in their student bodies. In fact, being Asian can be an admission hook at many schools. At nearly all colleges and universities, Asian-American applicants can tout their ethnicity and not hide it.

Action Plan

Asian Americans will significantly increase their admission success if they cast a wider net when applying to colleges.

Part III

Knowing Your Academic Choices

28

What's The Difference Between a College and a University?

When teenagers evaluate schools by size, they are missing a much larger factor that should go into their college admission decisions. When teens and parents ask how big a school is, they rarely ask what is its educational mission.

—The College Solution blog

What is the difference between a college and a university?

I've posed this question many times during presentations to parents and teenagers, and the simple query has stumped nearly everyone. It's rare that even one person raises his or her hand when I search around the room for someone who knows.

Why is this a tough question? Here's one explanation:

In this country, we use the words *college* and *university* interchangeably, so it's only natural that people think that they are the same thing. College is surely the most popular term. People routinely ask, "Where are you going to college?" You would never hear anybody ask, "Where are you going to university?"

Another reason why students and parents don't understand the difference between a college and a university is because too many families and high school counselors frame the question of where to go to college—see I'm doing it too—by focusing on size.

Students are routinely asked if they want to attend a big, medium, or small school. When educational choices are framed in terms of size, it's not surprising that teenagers express more interest in attending a medium or large university because they seem more attractive. If someone offered you a Hershey's Kiss or a Hershey's bar, wouldn't you rather have the bigger piece of chocolate?

Placing so much importance on size, however, can shortchange students in their search for good schools. When teenagers and their parents evaluate institutions by the number of students who attend, they are missing a much more important factor that should influence their selection process. What they overlook is the educational mission that distinguishes schools of different sizes. A school's mission is far more important than its size. There is a link, however, between a school's mission and size that is critical to consider when evaluating schools.

When you understand the educational missions of different types of institutions, you'll be in a better position to assemble a list of schools that will meet your educational goals.

Four Categories of Colleges and Universities

Among four-year schools, here is a thumbnail sketch of the four main types of institutions:

Research universities. The private and public schools in this category place a tremendous institutional focus on research and represent the most recognizable higher-ed brands.

Examples: University of Chicago, Harvard University, UCLA, Purdue University, University of Wisconsin, Rice University.

Master's degree or regional universities. These schools, which include private and state institutions, often don't have as great a focus on research and may offer degrees no higher than the master's level.

Examples: Villanova University, Elon University, Quinnipiac University, Butler University, New Mexico Institute of Mining and Technology, San Diego State University.

Liberal arts and baccalaureate colleges. These schools, which are primarily private, typically offer no graduate programs, which means undergraduates are the top priority at these institutions.

Examples: Amherst College, Kalamazoo College, SUNY College at Geneseo, Evergreen State College, Carleton College, College of Wooster, Colorado College.

Specialty schools. These schools focus on one area of expertise, such as art, music, business, or engineering.

Examples: Rhode Island School of Design, Juilliard School, Babson College, Boston Conservatory, Pratt Institute, Rose-Hulman Institute of Technology.

Why Do You Need to Know?

Unfortunately, the name of a school won't always tell you what kind of institution it is. Dartmouth College and Boston College, for instance, are universities. Emerson College is considered a master's-level university. Lawrence University, Illinois Wesleyan University, and University of Puget Sound are liberal arts colleges. In some cases, there are historical reasons for the designations.

Knowing the difference between a college and a university is critically important when a family begins exploring a teenager's options for after high school. In the next seven chapters, you'll learn more about the missions of these different types of schools.

Action Plan

Before getting serious about selecting schools, you should understand the difference between colleges and universities.

29

The Ivy League Myth

Students who apply to, and are accepted by, elite schools are likely to be high-achievers. High-achieving students are likely to have high earnings regardless of where they go to school.

—Alan B. Krueger, Princeton economist

A curious story appeared in *The New York Times* a few years ago about the university that's the academic equivalent of the Yankees.

The article captured the concerns of faculty, who worried that the teaching taking place at Harvard University wasn't meeting the school's own vaunted standards. In fact, a professor lamented that some undergraduates, after spending four years at Harvard, don't know a single faculty member well enough to ask for a letter of recommendation.

Hmmm.

One student who was interviewed by the *Times* reporter suggested that undergraduates ought to understand that Harvard's professors are too focused on research to put much effort into what happens in the classroom.

"You'd be stupid if you came to Harvard for the teaching," a Harvard senior and Rhodes scholar told the *Times* reporter. "You go to a liberal arts college for teaching. You come to Harvard to be around some of the greatest minds on earth."

And he had more to say: "I think many people (at Harvard) spend a great deal of their time in large lecture classes, have little direct contact with professors, and are frustrated by poorly trained teaching fellows."

Concerned about the quality of Harvard's undergraduate education, a small group of the university's professors cranked out a report that advocated for institutional changes that would place greater value on teaching. I'm sure the report made little if any impact on what happens on this sprawling campus. After all, Harvard's institutional angst about what occurs in its classrooms will neither dampen its star power among brilliant high school students nor prompt its professors to take teaching undergrads more seriously.

Pursuit of the Most Prestigious Universities

When many families begin their college search, they assume that the Ivy League owns a monopoly on the nation's best schools. The only ivy that most kids are going to come into contact with, however, will itch and require calamine lotion. Far fewer than a quarter of 1% of the nation's incoming college freshmen end up at the eight Ivy League universities.

While most smart teenagers don't even attempt to gain admittance into the nation's most exclusive schools, those who do can make themselves miserable in their frenetic quest for perfection. It's a given that students aiming for the Ivy League must ace a large number of Advanced Placement or International Baccalaureate courses and maintain a stellar grade point average. Being the smartest kid in a high school hardly provides an admissions lock on these schools. Every year, Ivy League institutions reject many valedictorians.

Extremely high scores on the SAT or ACT are also a must to get into the Ivy League. Participating in meaningful extracurricular activities that show leadership qualities is another prerequisite. Of course, the application must be flawless and the application essay inspiring.

Even teenagers who can check off all those boxes can almost always expect a rejection letter. Getting in is nearly impossible for students who aren't born to the right parents. The Ivy League schools favor students of celebrities, alumni, rich potential donors, and recruited athletes. (See Chapter 24, "The Legacy Hook.")

Despite the lousy odds, bright, ambitious students continue to apply because they believe that gaining entry into one of these eight schools will just about guarantee success in their future careers. Outsiders marvel at the networking opportunities, the brilliant professors (even if undergrads rarely even encounter them), and the prestige and exclusivity of these storied campuses.

Everybody already knows this. That's probably why when I wrote a post on April Fool's Day for my college blog at CBS MoneyWatch that suggested that Princeton had rejected all its applicants so it could become more exclusive than Harvard, my editor (a Penn grad) didn't immediately dismiss it as a joke.

Ivy League Grads Versus Everybody Else

While this will seem sacrilegious to students caught up by Ivy ambitions, here is some advice: You don't have to sacrifice your high school years in pursuit of the good life later.

Believe it or nor, undergrads who earn an Ivy League degree do not fare any better financially or in their careers than other gifted students who earn their degrees elsewhere. The Ivy League does not possess a monopoly on graduate success. Two highly regarded studies trashed the conventional wisdom that Ivy League grads enjoy an exclusive lock on the good life.

Researching the Ivy League Advantage

In the first study, published in 2002, two economists, Alan B. Krueger, a Princeton economist, and Stacy Dale, a senior researcher at Mathematica Policy Research, compared one-year earnings of students who had graduated from Ivy League schools in 1976 with bright teenagers who had gained admission to Ivy League schools but opted to attend elsewhere. The earnings of the two groups of graduates were nearly identical. The research strongly suggested that it wasn't the Ivy League institutions, but the students themselves that made the difference in their future success.

In 2011, the same economists released a more powerful and convincing study on the same subject. The researchers revisited what had happened to the two groups of students who started college in 1976 and were now middle aged. They discovered that the salary parity remained.

The researchers also compared the earnings of Ivy League graduates who began college in 1989 with students who had applied to Ivy League institutions but had been *rejected* by all of them. The spurned applicants, however, possessed the same high SAT scores as those who attended the Ivies. When the economists traced the earnings of both sets of graduates, they also were nearly identical.

So what does this research dramatically illustrate? It's not the Ivy League institutions that provide their graduates with an earnings boost. It's hard to make that argument when brilliant students who were rejected from these schools fared just as well in their careers. Rather, it's the students themselves who make the difference. Bright, ambitious students who aim high are more likely to do well no matter where they earn their bachelor's degree. The notable exceptions are minorities, as well as low-income students from less-educated families, who do greatly benefit from an Ivy League education.

It's probably asking too much for families bent on getting their kids into the Ivy League to accept that these schools don't represent the only ticket to a prosperous career. If they did, however, their children might be able to enjoy their teenage years.

Bottom Line

Many schools scattered across the country will provide an education that is as good as or superior to the one they'd receive at the most elite East Coast schools.

You can find the researchers' latest study on Ivy League wages by Googling its title, "Estimating the Return to College Selectivity over the Career Using Administrative Earning Data."

Action Plan

Do not assume that an Ivy League pedigree is required to succeed professionally.

30

What Is a Research University?

What do undergraduates get out of the research university?
Among many things, you get to be taught by faculty who, in
principle, are doing the same thing that you are doing. How
can a faculty member ask an undergraduate to take the risk
in learning new things without doing so himself? And since
students sometimes fail to learn, faculty have to be willing to
run the risk of their own similar failure.

—Brandeis University, commencement speech

Research universities are the best-known higher-ed institutions
in the country.

If you took a look at the top 25 schools in the latest national university rankings from *US News & World Report*, just about any American would recognize these schools. The list includes Stanford, Duke,
UCLA, MIT, Columbia, and Cornell—lots of heavy hitters.

Teenagers and their parents dream about going to research universities, whether it's a state flagship such as the University of Virginia
or University of North Carolina or a private university such as the
University of Chicago or Georgetown University, because they enjoy
stellar reputations. Wearing a sweatshirt from Princeton or Vanderbilt suggests that the owner must be smart indeed to earn admission
into such exclusive clubs.

For all the attention that these schools command, the vast majority of Americans do not attend them. When you add up all the public
and private nonprofit postsecondary institutions in this country—two-
year and four-year degree programs—research universities represent

less than 8% of the total, according to the Carnegie Foundation for the Advancement of Teaching.

Beyond their reputation, exclusivity, and, in some cases, their athletic records, I'd argue that families know very little about how private and public research universities operate. If I asked teenagers who are aiming for Harvard to name five of the school's academic strengths, I bet they'd be stumped.

Before teenagers apply to research universities, they need to understand what the missions of these institutions are and where undergraduates fit in.

The Missions of Research Universities

Research is highly prized. Research is the No. 1 priority of these universities. The most important job for professors at these august institutions is conducting research, which is principally how the faculty earn tenure and boost their income. Generating research brings in revenue and prestige to the faculty and the universities.

The academics at these institutions are more likely to be involved in cutting-edge research and to have become respected experts in their field. Star professors are attracted to research universities, which tend to have the finest laboratories and facilities. The professor giving the astronomy or chemistry lecture could be the very person who wrote the textbook. In addition to permanent faculty, research universities are better able to attract highly regarded authorities at the top of their field to teach for a semester or to give talks. You will learn much more about universities and research in the next chapter.

Training graduate students. Graduate students represent the second priority of a research university. Educating graduate students who will be the next PhDs is more labor intensive than teaching undergrads since these advanced students attend seminar classes and work one-on-one with academic advisors.

Teaching undergraduates. Teaching undergraduates is the No. 3 priority. If I had to summarize in one sentence how professors at research universities regard undergrads, this would be it: They're not that into you.

Professors tend to view undergraduates as impeding their research and thus often try to avoid or minimize their time with them. You can find this phenomenon, by the way, at public and private research universities. Undergrads at the Ivy League institutions, for instance, face the same issues with professor priorities. (See Chapter 29, "The Ivy League Myth.")

Graduate students typically have the most contact with undergraduates. A professor—perhaps one of those research stars—might provide the lectures for a class, but it's the grad students who grade the assignments, run the sections/labs, and communicate with the undergraduates.

Size of classes. Introductory classes at research universities can consist of hundreds of students. At some research universities, upper-level classes will have a small number of students while at others, the classes can contain 100 or more students.

Large classes require that learning remains passive. Students listen to a teacher, but there is little or no opportunity for them to engage actively in the classroom. Students do typically get a chance for discussion in section classes, but graduate students normally teach them.

Whether the classroom numbers are low enough for undergrads to participate can vary not only by university, but also within majors at institutions. Students, for instance, who are interested in less popular majors, may enjoy small classes and develop meaningful relationships with their professors.

Research universities have more money. Public and private research universities enjoy more resources than most other schools. In fact, the more elite the institution is, the more money there usually is to spend. As a general rule, the higher a university's standardized test scores and admission selectivity, the greater the spending per student.

While state flagships across the country are struggling with their budgets, they are still better off financially than the public universities farther down the food chain. Meanwhile, the most elite private research universities have seemed nearly immune to the pressures that their public peers are experiencing because they can raise their prices without worrying that they will discourage applicants. There will always be a demand from rich students to attend schools like Yale, Rice, and Emory. And, by the way, the majority of students who attend public and private research universities are affluent.

There clearly is an advantage to attending a school with a large endowment. According to a Georgetown University study, the students in the wealthiest 10% of institutions pay 20 cents in tuition and fees for every $1 spent on them versus students attending community colleges who spend 78 cents for every dollar spent on their education.

Higher graduation rates. Another practical consequence of attending these institutions is that their students are more likely to graduate in four years. The average graduation rate at elite private research universities is the highest of any category. The average grad rate of private research institutions is greater than public flagship universities, but the flagship grad rates will be superior to less selective state schools.

Let's compare, for instance, the graduation rate at the University of North Carolina, Chapel Hill (72%) with Western Carolina State (26.5%) or Fayetteville State (12.8%), or the University of Illinois at Urbana-Champaign (64.8%) versus 22.8% for Northern Illinois University or 24.1% for Southern Illinois University Carbondale.

Greater offering of majors and classes. Research universities can offer hundreds of degree programs. If you aren't sure what major you want, the university will probably have it once you figure that out.

To keep the universities academically manageable, they are divided into schools such as the schools or colleges of business, engineering, law, education, music, agriculture, medicine, nursing, journalism, and arts and sciences. Getting into some of these universities doesn't guarantee that you will be admitted into the school or college that you desire.

Largest playground. Beyond the academic offerings, research universities offer a bounty of social opportunities with clubs, entertainment, and sporting events. Students who hate the thought of attending a school that's the same size as their high school are attracted to schools with tens of thousands of students. On game days, the school spirit at universities with big-time sports can be infectious.

Does the university have an honors college? For the smartest students, the existence of honors colleges represents one of the most attractive benefits of attending a research university. An honors college tries to make an institution more personal by offering perks to the best students. The benefits can include seminar classes, priority registration, better academic advising, and special dorms.

Quite a few public universities, in particular, offer honors colleges. One of the more cynical reasons for the trend is to capture highly desirable students who might otherwise attend private schools. It's definitely worth checking into who qualifies for this special treatment.

Who is best suited for a research university? Undergraduates can flourish at research universities, but it helps to be an extrovert. These are the students who are more likely to possess the moxie to try to engage their professors. Research has suggested that the best educational experiences have happened not in classrooms, but during interactions with professors outside the classroom. It also helps to be brilliant. Often only the top students have any chance of working with professors in research projects.

Action Plan

Having meaningful access to professors is often tougher at research universities.

If you are an introvert, attending a research university might not be the best choice.

31

What University Professors Do

Many students cannot imagine going to speak with a professor in his or her office. At most universities, a student is likely to be unknown to the professor and would expect to feel like a nuisance, a distraction from more important work.

—William Pannapacker, associate professor of English, Hope College

Among professors, the freedom to pursue research is practically considered a birthright. I once talked to a friend of mine, who is a chemistry professor at a highly ranked university, about academics' preoccupation with research. He summed up his motivation along with that of his peers this way: "I'm not paid to teach, I'm paid to do research."

What's fascinating about this research focus is that it didn't used to interfere with what many families wrongly assume is the No. 1 priority of universities—teaching students. I was surprised when I read a history of the University of California, Berkeley, and discovered that earlier in the 20th century, professors at this esteemed flagship conducted their research in their spare time and spent their workweeks teaching students.

Those days will never return, but I don't think it's too much to ask that the academic pursuits of professors be balanced with the rights of undergraduates to obtain a decent education. Students have clearly lost in this tug of war and with disastrous consequences.

Why Research Is King

Why do universities revere research?

Money—lots of it—primarily explains the research obsession on campuses. Successful research proposals can attract grants from the federal government, private industry, and elsewhere that can help keep on the lights. These dollars are pumped into teacher salaries and into gorgeous research facilities that will impress potential students and their families. There is even an exclusive, highly coveted club—the Association of American Universities—for institutions positioned at the top of the research heap. Research is so valued that elite universities—or wannabes—pursue star researchers as if they were rock stars. Ironically, the professors with the most stellar reputations, including the Nobel Prize laureates, are the academics least likely to teach.

When evaluating universities and faculty, it's much easier to measure research output. The number of papers that Professor A produces can be compared to Professor B or to all the candidates applying for a professorial spot. While it's a snap to measure research outputs of professors in the prevailing publish-or-perish environment, it's much trickier to evaluate whether professors are good teachers. How do you know if the organic chemistry or economics professor is an effective teacher?

While some academic research, particularly in the sciences, is valuable, too much of it is Mickey Mouse. Mark Bauerlein, an English professor at Emory University, for instance, has written persuasively about the questionable and/or redundant research that humanities departments are producing. Over the past five decades, the number of papers that professors of language and literature generate has soared from 13,000 to 72,000 a year. It doesn't seem to discourage academics that few are reading their stuff.

Indoctrinating Grad Students

The emphasis on research actually begins long before a person snags his first professor gig. When idealistic young Americans are applying to graduate schools, they are expected to emphasize their love of scholarship. Mentioning a passion for teaching in a graduate school application can actually hurt applicants.

Once in graduate programs, future academics are not taught how to be teachers. Their instruction focuses on the discipline that they are pursuing. In his excellent book, *The Thinking Student's Guide to College: 75 Tips For Getting a Better Education*, Andrew Roberts, a professor at Northwestern University, provides this take:

> Even if your main goal remains to become a teacher, you will still get almost no training in teaching at graduate school. Yes, you will be asked to serve as a teaching assistant and possibly even teach your own class, but more than likely you will be thrown into your first teaching situation with little prior preparation. You will have to learn to teach on your own and you will sometimes even be encouraged not to go the extra mile. In short, don't expect to be trained as a teacher in doctoral programs. This may be a scandal and probably should be changed, but it is the way things are.

How Students Get Shortchanged

Why should you care if professors are preoccupied with their research? Because it can hurt your child's chances of getting a decent education.

With scholarship valued above all else at research universities, undergraduate instruction is too often left to graduate students, adjuncts, and part-time instructors, who may be teaching at multiple schools to make ends meet. In this type of environment, forming bonds with professors is far more difficult. As the relationship between professors and students has declined, so too has student engagement.

When students don't feel connected to their professors, it's easy to argue that they aren't going to make as much of an effort. And there is widespread evidence that many students are skating through school rather than squeezing the most out of their college experience. In Chapter 36, "Are Students Really Learning?," I share statistics that suggest that more than one out of three students graduate from college without showing any improvement in critical reasoning and thinking, as well as writing.

Professors who wrote a pair of commentaries published in *Nature* and *Science* magazines lamented how universities have devalued the importance of undergraduate instruction and argued for a better balance between teaching and research. They also urged schools to take teaching ability into consideration when awarding professors tenure and help faculty improve their teaching skills.

Economic forces might end up driving more professors back into the classrooms, particularly at public universities. With state financial support continuing to dwindle, universities are exploring ways to live with less, and making professors actually teach is a no-brainer.

Action Plan

When evaluating universities, explore how much interaction students have with their professors.

Particularly at state universities, class sizes can number in the hundreds of students, but ask what the class sizes will be when a student begins taking courses in his or her major. The answer could vary from department to department within a school.

32

The Beauty of Liberal Arts Colleges

I am a confessed enthusiast and supporter of the small, selective liberal arts colleges. My pulse quickens when I see students from Carleton, Haverford, and Williams who have applied to our PhD program.

—Thomas R. Cech, chemistry professor at University of Colorado and Nobel Prize winner

I ate lunch once with an extremely successful West Coast businesswoman whose children and husband graduated from Yale University. Her husband is an involved Yale alum and donor, and I got the impression that there was never any doubt that their children would head to New Haven after high school.

Before the waiter had handed us our menus, my lunch guest blurted out that her children might have been better off attending a liberal arts college. Without any prompting from me, she explained her reasoning. Her children had graduated from Yale without forming relationships with their professors, and their diplomas hadn't led to the sort of jobs that you'd expect Ivy League grads to command. At a liberal arts college, she observed, her children would have attended small classes and gotten to know their professors in an intimate learning environment that might have led to a better experience.

I'm sure most families would find the woman's discontent strange. Yale, after all, is a higher-ed alpha dog. What's more, I think most people would find the woman's admiration of liberal arts colleges puzzling. Few Americans know what liberal arts colleges are, much less why they could be a superior choice to an Ivy League school.

Among the top 25 liberal arts colleges in this country, according to *US News & World Report*, are such institutions as Scripps, Davidson, Hamilton, Carleton, Macalester, Bates, and Washington and Lee. You might have heard of these excellent schools because you're interested enough in the subject to read this book, but the typical person hasn't.

While the anonymity is exasperating to liberal arts colleges, it's not surprising. There are thousands of institutions of higher learning in this country, but it's been estimated that only 3% of college students attend liberal arts colleges.

Before I share the advantages of liberal arts colleges, I should reveal my own bias. Like Thomas R. Cech, a liberal arts graduate (Grinnell) and a Nobel Prize laureate, whose quote graces the top of this chapter, I am an unapologetic advocate of these colleges. My daughter graduated from a liberal arts college (Juniata College), and my son attends one now (Beloit College).

Like most Americans with a bachelor's degree, I attended a state university (University of Missouri). Also like the majority of parents, my husband and I assumed that our children would also end up at a big state school. But as I mentioned in this book's introduction, when my daughter and I realized that that the school that she assumed she would attend (University of California, Berkeley) turned out to be unattainable, we fortuitously veered off on a path less traveled.

What Is a Liberal Arts College?

By their very nature, liberal arts colleges are small. While many have been growing in size incrementally for financial reasons, most have fewer than 2,500 students. The schools are committed to a residential learning environment where students typically live on campus for four years. This is in contrast to the vast majority of universities, where undergrads usually must move off campus after their freshman year.

The size of liberal arts colleges represents a distinct advantage to students. At these schools, students won't get stuck in lecture halls that could require TV monitors to see the professor. A few introductory courses, like Biology 101 or Psychology 101, might have 40 or 50 students, but nearly all the rest will typically contain 20 students or considerably fewer. In my daughter's first semester at Juniata, for instance, the professor thought there were too many students (16) enrolled in her conversational Spanish class, so he voluntarily split the class in two and taught back-to-back sessions just so his students could get more time speaking Spanish.

The Priorities of Liberal Arts Colleges

A distinctive mark of a liberal arts college is its dedication to undergraduates. The primary focus of the professors is teaching the undergrads, and, unlike the institutional priorities at universities, research comes second. Students don't have to compete with graduate students for attention because graduates students don't exist at the typical liberal arts college. Unlike at research universities, where a lousy professor who is a great researcher can receive tenure, a professor's teaching ability is of tantamount importance at a liberal arts college.

These colleges focus almost exclusively on the liberal arts and sciences. They offer majors in such disciplines as literature, languages, psychology, economics, political science, chemistry, physics, and math. Bowing to popular demand, many liberal arts college also offer business degrees. However, students who want to major in other vocational degrees, such as criminology, nursing, and occupational therapy, will have to look elsewhere. You can, however, find these types of majors at baccalaureate colleges, which you learn about later in the chapter.

It would probably be an understatement to note that the liberal arts are under siege. Parents, teenagers, and even some politicians believe that the liberal arts are hopelessly impractical. In berating the liberal arts, the governor of Florida once remarkably singled out anthropology as a worthless degree. Liberal arts colleges offer a lot of legitimate arguments to refute this assault on the liberal arts. Many desirable jobs require science and math ability, for which liberal arts colleges excel.

When employers are surveyed, here is what they routinely say they value: young Americans who can think clearly, write well, and who can stand up at a meeting and give a persuasive presentation. One of the missions of liberal arts colleges is to teach kids how to think, talk, and write. Don't all schools do that? Not necessarily. You can graduate from plenty of universities without writing essays or research papers. Who, after all, is going to grade 500 essays? In small class settings, liberal arts students are more likely to be required to write papers, give class presentations, and collaborate with their classmates and professors. You can't hide from the teachers at these schools.

In blockbuster research that was turned into a book, *Academically Adrift*, researchers concluded that more than a third of students in the study graduated from college without any growth in critical thinking, reasoning, or writing. The students at colleges and universities who exhibited the most improvement were those who majored in the liberal arts, while students enrolled in business, education, and communication programs learned the least.

Given the opportunity for a more intimate learning experience, it's not surprising that college professors, who are the ultimate insiders, are far more likely to send their children to liberal arts colleges. A study conducted by two Vanderbilt researchers revealed that the children of professors were about twice as likely to attend a liberal arts college than children of other affluent families, which for the purposes of the study were described as those earning more than $100,000 a year.

Graduate School Chances

One fear that families raise when exploring liberal arts colleges is expressed something like this: Wouldn't attending a liberal arts college hurt the chances of getting into graduate school? Or the flip side to that question is this: Don't you have to attend a prestigious university to get into graduate school?

Actually, students may increase their odds of being accepted to graduate school if they earn their bachelor's degree at a liberal arts college. On a per capita basis, for instance, liberal arts colleges produce twice as many students who earn a PhD in science than other institutions. That makes sense since students have more opportunities to work closely with their professors and receive impressive recommendations from their teachers, many of which graduated from highly regarded graduate programs.

While the average Joe hasn't heard of schools like Reed, Oberlin, St. John's, Kalamazoo, Bryn Mawr, and Wabash, graduate schools are well aware of the caliber of undergrads from these colleges who are eager to continue their education.

Reed College in Portland, Oregon, which pumps out future PhDs at a rate that no Ivy League institution can touch, has posted on its website a PhD scorecard that illustrates the success that some liberal arts colleges have enjoyed in getting their students into graduate school. The chart lists the colleges and universities that educate the most undergrads, as a percentage of their students, who go on to obtain their PhDs. The college obtained the figures from the National Science Foundation and the federal government's education database.

You can find the scorecards that Reed assembled by Googling "*Reed*" and "*PhD productivity*." Here are three of the tallies. (I identified the liberal arts institutions that don't contain "college" in their names.)

Most PhD Graduates, per capita, in all disciplines

1. California Institute of Technology
2. Harvey Mudd College
3. Reed College
4. Swarthmore College
5. Massachusetts Institute of Technology
6. Carleton College
7. Grinnell College
8. Bryn Mawr College
9. University of Chicago
10. Oberlin College

Most PhD Graduates, per capita, in English and Literature

1. Bard College at Simon's Rock
2. St. John's College
3. Amherst College
4. Yale University
5. Reed College
6. Swarthmore College
7. Bryn Mawr College
8. Wesleyan University (liberal arts college)
9. Williams College
10. Oberlin College

Most PhD Graduates, per capita, in Chemistry

1. Harvey Mudd College
2. California Institute of Technology
3. Wabash College
4. Reed College
5. New Mexico Institute of Mining & Technology
6. Carleton College
7. University of Minnesota, Morris (public liberal arts college)
8. College of Wooster
9. Kalamazoo College
10. Transylvania University (liberal arts college)

What's even more remarkable about the prominence of liberal arts colleges on the science lists is this: Many students major in other disciplines at liberal colleges, while students who attend schools like Cal Tech and MIT overwhelmingly expect to pursue careers in the sciences and engineering.

You can find a lengthy essay that Cech wrote that contrasts the science offerings for undergrads at colleges and universities by Googling its title, "Science at Liberal Arts Colleges: A Better Education?."

Finding Liberal Arts Colleges

Liberal arts colleges are scattered around the country, though they are in shorter supply in the West. You'll find a list by visiting the website of the Annapolis Group, which is an organization composed of 130 liberal arts colleges (www.collegenews.org/annapolis-group-member-colleges).

Another resource is *Colleges That Change Lives*, which is a book and website that share the same name. The late Loren Pope, a former education editor of *The New York Times*, wrote the book as a tribute to liberal arts colleges and highlights 40 specific institutions. After his newspaper days, Pope became a college counselor, but he was discouraged by the fixation on Ivy League schools because he believed that liberal arts colleges often provided as good, if not better, education.

Be warned that *Colleges That Change Lives*, which was most recently revised in 2006, is outdated, but you will obtain a great sense of what all liberal arts colleges offer by reading it. You can gather current information by visiting the website of Colleges That Change Lives (http://www.ctcl.org/). As a group, the 40 CTCL schools hold yearly events in cities across the country.

While I've focused in this chapter on private liberal arts colleges, there are also public versions of these institutions. Public liberal arts colleges are bigger—often 5,000 or so students—and they can offer grad programs, but these programs aren't as numerous as what you'd find at a university.

Some of these public liberal arts colleges possess more impressive graduation rates than research universities. For instance, the grad rate of the College of New Jersey (72.7%) and St. Mary's College of Maryland (71.3%) are superior to the grad rates of almost all public universities including such flagships as Penn State (62.1%) and University of California, Berkeley (66.3%). You can find the names of the nation's public liberal arts colleges at the Council of Public Liberal Arts Colleges (www.copc.org).

Liberal arts colleges aren't for everyone. Some teenagers will refuse to consider any college that is smaller than their own high schools and others might balk at considering any place that doesn't offer big-time sports programs, but the opportunities that liberal arts colleges offer are definitely worth a look.

Baccalaureate Colleges

The baccalaureate college is the other type of college. Of the two categories, liberal arts colleges are considered the most prestigious and selective, though there are exceptions, such as Cooper Union for the Advancement of Science and Art, the U.S. Coast Guard Academy, and the U.S. Air Force Academy.

Baccalaureate colleges also offer the liberal arts majors, but the majority of students at these public and private institutions select more vocational-oriented majors, such as nursing, allied health, education, parks and recreation, and business.

Examples of baccalaureate colleges include High Point University, Lebanon Valley College, Elizabethtown College, Dordt College, Tuskegee University, and California Maritime Academy. An excellent way to find schools in this category is to pick up a copy of *US News & World Report's* college rankings guide and look for the "Best Regional Colleges" category.

Action Plan

Rather than looking exclusively at universities, consider also exploring colleges.

33

What Is a Medium-Sized University?

If you look at American higher education from the outside in,
what does the country need from them? Our major deficits
are not on the research side but on the training of undergrads.

—Patrick M. Callan, former director of the National Center
for Public Policy and Higher Education

A few years ago, Cleveland State University decided it wanted to
make a name for itself by becoming known for its research. Cleveland State was never going to achieve the reputation that Ohio State
University or any other flagship enjoys, but it hoped to generate some
prestige wattage of its own by hiring professors with potential star
power.

With a stable of crackerjack academic researchers, the university's aim was to attract $50 million in yearly research grants. Research,
after all, is what drives reputation in university circles. To provide professors with more time to conduct their research, however, something
had to be sacrificed. Consequently, the urban university assigned
graduate students to take over more of the instruction in classrooms
and laboratories.

Cleveland State's goal to make a name for itself through its
research didn't pan out. In an article in *The Chronicle of Higher Education*, the president of the nonselective university stated what most
people would consider to be obvious: The school needed to focus on
educating undergraduates rather than pursuing an ambitious research
agenda.

When you look at Cleveland State's graduation stats, you might wonder why on earth this institution ever diverted attention away from its undergrads. A mere 7% of full-time students graduate in four years. Only 29% manage to graduate in six years. Dreadful stats.

Why am I sharing the misadventures of Cleveland State? Most students in this country attend public universities not much different from Cleveland State. While public research universities enjoy the best reputations in their states—and often superior athletic teams— most students head off to medium-sized public universities.

Public Regional Universities

These schools are considered regional universities, and you'll also hear them referred to as master's degree institutions. That's because at these universities, there are few if any PhD programs. Instead, the graduate programs at these universities focus on master's degrees. These schools offer degrees in the liberal arts and sciences, but they also provide popular career-oriented degrees such as business, nursing, education, criminal justice, kinesiology, engineering, and communications. They won't provide as many programs as an intensive research university, but really how many do you need?

Many of these regional public institutions were founded in the 19th century as colleges dedicated to educating schoolteachers. The primary mission was later expanded to educate undergrads in other disciplines, but eventually the regional universities caught the research bug. Just like Cleveland State, many of these institutions began putting more of an emphasis on faculty research production.

One of the realities of regional public institutions, compared to flagships, is less funding. The flagships get to eat at the state budget trough first, and the regional schools typically make due with the scraps. Less funding is a major reason why master's-level public universities often generate low four-year grad rates. While some higher-ed observers will suggest that the flagships enjoy higher grad track records because they attract smarter students, studies have shown that the funding (or lack of it) is the prime reason for inferior grad rates. It is a fact, however, that the admission requirements imposed by regional public universities are typically lower than those of the prestigious flagships.

Private Master's-Level Universities

Many private institutions also fall into the regional or master's degree category. Numerous Catholic universities, for instance, fit into this category, including Villanova, Seattle, Santa Clara, Loyola Marymount, Marquette, Creighton, St. Louis University, Salve Regina, Fairfield, Xavier, and Gonzaga universities. Non-Catholic, mid-sized institutions include Ithaca, Hood, and Emerson colleges, as well as Chapman, Butler, Quinnipiac, Drake, Belmont, and Elon universities.

These private institutions offer the same sorts of degree programs that their public counterparts provide: the traditional science/liberal arts offerings along with career-oriented degrees. These schools can be popular with students who want to attend a university but not one that is too large. Many of these schools have student bodies between 7,000 and 12,000 rather than tens of thousands.

Evaluating Master's-Level Universities

I'd argue that medium-sized universities are the hardest to evaluate. You know that the primary mission of flagships and other research-intensive universities, such as the Ivy League institutions, is research and graduate education. In contrast, colleges are dedicated to educating undergrads. But at medium-sized universities, the commitment to undergrad education versus research varies. Trying to get some sense of where a particular institution resides on this continuum can be challenging, but certainly worth the effort.

When researching public or private regional universities, you should look at what the typical class sizes are in general and also in your major. You'll also want to get a sense of what kind of access you have to professors. At private schools, you will probably have opportunities for smaller classes, but you shouldn't assume that this will always be true. Great sources to find candid answers about a university's dedication to teaching and undergraduates will be current students or recent alumni.

You can certainly receive an excellent education at a master's-level university. As with all types of higher-ed institutions, some schools will offer a better education than others. Some departments will excel, and others will stink within the same school. You most definitely should not assume that the education you receive at a master's-level school would be inferior to what you would experience at a research juggernaut.

In writing this chapter, I am reminded of the experience of one of my daughter's best friends in high school. Kristina attended California State University Monterey Bay and graduated with a degree in environmental science. She enjoyed small classes, she adored her science professors, and through her school mentor she found fantastic internships in her field, including the renowned Monterey Bay Aquarium. Could Kristina have had a better educational experience at the state's flagship—University of California, Berkeley? Not likely.

Action Plan

When evaluating master's-level universities, try to get a sense of whether the institutions are more focused on research or training undergraduates.

34

Why Community Colleges Are Popular

The first concern of the research university is, unsurprisingly, research. Community colleges, by contrast are far more focused on teaching, and some are doing it better than even the most esteemed four-year institutions.

—Kevin Carey, policy director at Education Sector

With college prices continuing to climb, community colleges are growing in popularity. Teenagers who never would have considered a community college as a serious option are changing their minds.

Nearly 44% of all undergraduates attend community colleges. If you don't find that statistic surprising, surely this one is: One out of every seven college students in this country attends a community college in California.

With roughly 1,200 community colleges in existence, campuses are located within commuting distance of more than 90% of Americans.

The relatively low price of community colleges is an obvious draw. The tuition at the nation's typical community college is about a third of the price of a four-year state university.

Looking at the pricing, many people assume that lower prices automatically translate into lower quality, but that's not true. Community colleges provide a more personalized education than what's offered at many highly regarded state universities, where a great deal of instruction takes place in lecture halls. Community colleges allow students to take the same required general education classes as students at state universities, but in a far more intimate setting.

With smaller classes, community college students face better odds of getting to know their professors in a way that an underclassman enrolled in introductory classes at a university rarely experiences. In fact, community college professors teach their own classes unlike many of their counterparts at four-year universities, where research is their primary job. Students at community colleges can be in a better position to elicit their teachers' help.

Some students see community colleges as a temporary pit stop because their grades weren't good enough for their dream schools. Through open admission policies, community colleges routinely admit anyone with a high school diploma or GED regardless of a student's standardized test scores or high school transcript.

Community colleges, however, are also becoming more attractive to high school graduates who normally would move directly to a four-year school. To attract these students, an increasing number of schools are offering honors classes. Some of these schools belong to the National Collegiate Honors Council, which sets standards for honors programs at two- and four-year institutions. You can find schools in the council by visiting its website at www.nchchonors.org.

I've been encountering more affluent parents who are curious about sending their children to community colleges. Many of these parents haven't saved enough money for four-year institutions, but they also wonder why they should sacrifice financially when their children could take the same general-ed classes with fewer students and for less money.

The Downside of Community Colleges

The biggest rap against the typical community college is that it's a Bermuda Triangle. Many students who start at community colleges end up disappearing into the system. Most community college students never earn their associate's degree much less move on to finish their education at a four-year institution.

There are various reasons for the dismal track record. For starters, not all students are interested in earning an associate's degree.

Some students are focused on obtaining a vocational credential. Also, many students juggle work, family, and classes, which makes it harder to slog through the requirements.

Another roadblock are remedial courses. Since community colleges accept all comers, they routinely require students to take placement tests. Those who don't fare well end up assigned to remedial classes for which they receive no college credit.

A *Washington Monthly* article, which suggested that community colleges consign too many students to remedial courses, called the remedial placement process "ground zero for college non-completion in America."

Here is another reason: It's human nature to meet others' expectations. If classmates work hard and aim for good grades, you are more likely to do the same. Surrounded by less-motivated students, it's going to be harder to stay serious about your studies. If a community college doesn't expect a lot out of its students, it won't get it.

Difficulty transferring credits is another real concern of community college students. When you do move to a different school, you want all your credits to move with you. See Chapter 51, "Getting Credit for Your Work," for more on this subject.

Finally, there is the social aspect of college life. Some students hesitate to attend a two-year school because they want to experience living on a campus. Some community colleges, however, offer dorms, including some two-year private junior colleges.

The Best Community Colleges

For motivated students, exemplary community colleges are scattered across the country, and some of the finest are celebrated each year by *Washington Monthly* when it releases its own honor roll.

"Students at the top community colleges," the magazine observed, "are more likely than their research university peers to get prompt feedback from instructors, work with other students on projects in class, make class presentations, and contribute to class discussions.... At the best community colleges, teaching comes first."

Community College Survey of Student Engagement

Washington Monthly produces its list by looking at community college graduation rates as well as a treasure trove of data from the Community College Survey of Student Engagement (CCSSE), which is based at the University of Texas, Austin. Years ago, educators at the University of Texas developed national benchmarks for academic excellence at community colleges. The survey was created to determine how well schools were meeting the benchmarks.

The survey includes questions about institutional practices and student behaviors that are thought to be highly correlated with student learning and retention. The CCSSE asks students to fill out the survey at their schools that touch upon these five areas:

- Active and collaborative learning
- Student effort
- Academic challenge
- Student-faculty interaction
- Support for learners

Here are some of the questions posted on the survey's website that students are asked:

Active and Collaborative Learning

- Did you ask questions in class or contribute to class discussions?
- Did you make a class presentation?
- Did you work with other students on projects during class?

Student-Faculty Interaction

- Did you discuss grades or assignments with a teacher?
- Did you talk to a teacher or advisor about career plans?
- Did you discuss ideas from your readings or classes with instructors outside of class?

Academic Challenge

- How many papers or reports of any length did you write?
- How often did you work harder than you thought you could to meet an instructor's standards or expectations?

Not all community colleges participate in the survey, but you can find the yearly results of the two-year schools that do on the CCSSE's website at www.ccsse.org. Ideally colleges are participating so they can determine what's working and what's not in educating their students.

Action Plan

A community college can provide a more intimate and inexpensive learning experience for students.

When evaluating a school, see whether it has participated in the Community College Survey of Student Engagement and, if so, check the results.

35

Nine Ways to Generate College Ideas

"I can tell you the kind of school I'd really like," my son told the college counselor, with an air of finality. "I want to go to a place where I can go to a football game, take off my shirt, paint my chest, and major in beer."

—Andrew Ferguson, author of *Crazy U: One Dad's Crash Course in Getting His Kid Into College*

It's almost always a smart idea to cast a wider net when exploring schools, but how do you do that? Keep reading to discover eight ways that can help you conduct an intelligent search.

1. Use college search engines.

College search engines can assist you in locating schools by using a variety of different criteria.

Surely the biggest is the federal College Navigator search engine, which is fueled by the U.S. Department of Education's monster database. Just Google *"College Navigator"* to find the website. To locate potential schools, you can select criteria such as private and public institutions, costs, majors, admission selectivity, religious affiliation, sports, and more. Click on the icon of the U.S. map on the home page, and you'll be able to designate the states and/or regions that you'd like to explore.

You'll find other helpful search engines at the websites of COLLEGEdata, College Board's BigFuture, Princeton Review, and Student Advisor.

2. Use the rankings.

As I mention in Chapter 37, "What's Wrong With *US News & World Report*'s College Rankings," *US News & World Report*'s rankings are flawed, but they can provide a tip sheet for families looking for schools beyond the best known.

I am more impressed by *Forbes* magazine's college rankings (see Chapter 39, "College Rankings: An Alternative"). While you can find the magazine's annual list by Googling *"Forbes"* and *"college rankings,"* I prefer looking at the lineup on the website of The Center for College Affordability and Productivity (www.centerforcollegeaffordability.org), which generates the lists. On the site, you can find the best colleges list as well as other lists broken down by region, type of school, and more.

3. Check out College Results Online (www.collegeresults.org).

College Results Online, a service of the Education Trust, is a great source to check any school's graduation rates (see Chapter 41, "Staying in College Too Long"). You can also use the site to generate lists of comparable schools. For instance, if you are interested in Drake University in Iowa, you can click the Similar Schools link and get the names of comparable universities. When I did this, I generated a list that included Butler, Xavier, Fairfield, Chapman, Seattle Pacific, Gonzaga, and Belmont universities.

4. Check out Unigo (www.unigo.com) and College Prowler (www.collegeprowler.com).

Unigo provides comments and videos from current students who share their opinions about their schools. The students' comments are valuable because the schools can't whitewash them. You can also find student reviews of schools on the website of College Prowler.

5. Zinch and Cappex.

These free online college matchmakers have borrowed features from Facebook that should appeal to teenagers. On both sites, for instance, teens can create their own profiles and showcase their talents, activities, passions and goals to an audience of hundreds of colleges and universities.

Colleges use the search function to look for promising applicants whether they are violinists, dancers, basketball guards or students from distant time zones. A traditional way that colleges have found teenagers is through the makers of the SAT and ACT, which sell names to schools. In contrast, the matchmaker sites allow students to take an active role in reaching out to colleges rather than waiting to be discovered.

6. Use guidebooks.

The annual *Fiske Guide to Colleges* and *The Princeton Review's Best Colleges* provide backgrounds on hundreds of schools.

7. Head to College Majors 101 (www.collegemajors101.com).

This is a wonderful resource to research college majors. For instance, what can you do with an environmental science degree? On this site, you can also find schools that offer particular majors, as well as view major-specific videos that schools create. In addition, you can generate ideas by discovering what student associations and publications are linked to particular majors.

8. Use CollegeWeekLive (www.collegeweeklive.com).

This website, which bills itself as the world's largest college fair, connects hundreds of schools with students through live streaming video presentations. You can find the calendar of events by heading to its website.

9. Visit schools virtually.

Many schools provide virtual tours on their websites. You can also check out videos of lots of schools at YOUniversityTV.com.

Action Plan

Use the resources in this chapter to help generate a list of promising college prospects. Being creative when formulating college lists is more likely to lead to an affordable bachelor's degree.

Part IV

Evaluating the Academics

36

Are Students Really Learning?

Colleges and universities, for all the benefits they bring, accomplish far less for their students than they should.

—Derek Bok, former president of Harvard University

Much of the zany hoopla surrounding college involves getting in. But what happens when the warm-up to college is finished and the main event arrives? After students settle in at college, do they learn much?

This might seem like a weird question to ask when a bachelor's degree appears more coveted today than ever. A college degree is the currency that society—or at least employers—use to determine whether a person possesses enough intellectual heft to create an ad campaign, negotiate a business deal, or teach a sixth grader what DNA is. Without this credential, the prospects of a satisfying and well-paying career seem to nearly disintegrate.

But here's the thing: The diplomas that many students are *earning* are a j-o-k-e. A stunning number of students are graduating without learning much of anything.

It's a national scandal, but colleges and universities have gotten away with ripping off their customers for years because parents like you and me have not been complaining. Everybody just assumes that the age-old arrangement that occurs every fall is working. We hand our teenagers and cash (often borrowed) over to the university and in return we get our child back—smarter, wiser, and employable—after the commencement ceremony. It's a win-win scenario, except it now appears, in too many instances, to be a lose (us) - win (schools) scenario.

A Higher-Ed Bombshell

While higher-ed reformers have been trying to guilt institutions into caring more about undergraduate education for a long time, it took a slim book titled *Academically Adrift: Limited Learning on College Campuses*, written by a pair of academics, to bring the crisis to center stage. The book dropped a big fat stink bomb on the higher-ed industry, and the stench shows no sign of dissipating.

What Richard Arum, a professor of sociology at New York University, and Josipa Roksa, an assistant professor of sociology at the University of Virginia, did was use a highly respected test—the Collegiate Learning Assessment (CLA)—to help answer the question of whether college students are making academic progress. The CLA, which you can learn more about at the website of Council for Aid to Education (www.cae.org), the sponsoring organization, is impressive in part because of what it doesn't measure. It isn't like an Advanced Placement test that aims to assess the facts that you've temporarily parked in your brain, such as the political and economic events that led to the French Revolution. It also doesn't play mind games with you like the SAT, which is an aptitude test.

The CLA, which is not subject specific, requires that test takers use the kind of thinking, problem solving, and writing skills that we would expect our college graduates to possess. Here's an example of a typical CLA assignment:

> The test takers must assume that they work for an electronics instrument company, which is grappling with whether to buy a small plane for its sales force. Shortly before the purchase was to be made, the favored model was involved in a crash. Should the company go ahead and buy the plane or bail? To answer this, the test taker is given many documents to review including press accounts of the crash, a federal accident report on in-flight breakups of single-engine planes, and an industry magazine article comparing this plane with others. The student must write a memo that addresses many questions including whether the data supports the claim that the plane's wings could lead to more accidents and whether the company should buy the plan.

The CLA is considered a state-of-the art test that measures critical thinking, reasoning, writing, and problem solving, which is why the research findings that led to the publication of *Academically Adrift* are so alarming. The academics took a look at the CLA results for 2,300 statistically representative undergrads who were enrolled in a diverse collection of 24 undisclosed colleges and universities from 2005 to 2009.

Of all the findings, here are the two biggies:

- 45% of the students made no gains in learning during their first two years in college.
- 36% of the students managed to graduate from college without learning much of anything.

Why Aren't Students Learning Enough?

Academically Adrift is an indictment of an industry that has been more preoccupied with attracting students and entertaining them than providing their customers with a meaningful learning experience. The study results naturally lead to this question: Why aren't more students learning?

Lowered expectations are certainly a major culprit. Many professors do not demand much from their students. About a third of the students in the study didn't take any courses that required more than 40 pages of reading a week. In addition, half didn't take a single course that required more than 20 pages of writing in a semester. More than a third of students spent less than five hours a week studying.

It's been far easier and lucrative for institutions to devote energy and money into things that can be measured and exploited by marketers. Erecting a breathtaking student union or a palace for the business school will bring more paying customers in the door. And families are more likely to ignore institutions that haven't made this a priority. In chasing prestige, universities are just as eager to hire the hottest researchers even if these stars are allergic to undergrads.

In contrast, spending time and money developing learning standards and revamping curriculum that will lead students to graduate with the skills they need to succeed in life is much tougher and largely unappreciated. Even professors who desire to be better teachers don't get the support they need from their institutions. I'm sure some administrators ask themselves, "Why put in the effort, when *US News & World Report* won't give a damn?"

Frankly, professors and students have called a truce on many campuses. The faculty doesn't expect too much out of students and give mostly A's and B's. Appreciative of the lighter workload, students reward the professors with good teacher evaluations. The arrangement results in professors having less work to grade and more time to devote to their own research, and students get to enjoy more free time too. Depressing, huh?

The *Academically Adrift* results weren't entirely grim. Students who majored in the liberal arts and sciences demonstrated significantly higher gains in the test. That's not surprising since liberal arts and sciences (think subjects like philosophy, chemistry, math, and French) are more academically demanding than many vocational ones, which are among the most popular with today's college students. Only 40% of college students are liberal arts majors. The students who fared the poorest were studying business, education, social work, and communications, which you could argue are among the easiest majors.

Measuring Student Learning

You have every right to wonder how you could possibly know whether students face a fighting chance of receiving a top-notch education at a particular school. Getting answers will be easier in the future because technological advances are beginning to make it possible to measure student outcomes. PayScale, a popular online resource for salaries, for instance, collects and publishes employment data for graduates of individual schools. PayScale's employment figures are self reported, but state governments have the ability to collect this information—a growing number are—and make it publicly available.

There is no reason why salary figures for graduates of all higher-ed institutions shouldn't be accessible to everyone.

The federal government has also been making increasing noise about pushing colleges and universities to be more responsive to undergrads. The higher-ed world has been stewing about the possibility of the government demanding accountability in return for the billions of dollars it pumps into the system every year in the form of grants, loans, and tax credits. But why, for example, should dropout factories that graduate an alarmingly low percentage of their students continue to feed at the federal trough without any repercussions?

With accountability still much more of a dream than a reality, it's going to be difficult to know whether the schools on your teenager's list take their role as educators seriously. In fact, at any given school, one department might be doing a bang-up job compared to another one that's up a flight of steps.

As you'll learn later in Chapter 40, there are high-impact practices that studies suggest increase a student's chances of thriving academically. You are more likely to find many of these practices at liberal arts colleges, which by their very nature are in a better position to deliver because they exist to serve undergrads in small, intimate settings. (Only 3% of students, however, attend liberal arts colleges.) You can't assume, however, that all colleges do an admirable job anymore than you can assume that universities with their research missions are shortchanging their students.

Tuning College Disciplines

If you look, you will find promising developments across the country. For example, thanks to grants from the Lumina Foundation, one of the true good guys in the higher-ed world, Utah's state universities have been working to improve their students' educational experience by determining what knowledge and skills they should demonstrate before graduating in specific disciplines. The process is called tuning. Utah's trailblazing public universities now have academic standards in place for history and physics majors, and they are tackling the disciplines of elementary education and math education. One part of the process had project participants survey employers of recent graduates—General Electric and the Air Force among others—to discover what knowledge and skills are necessary for science careers.

Lumina has also funded tuning pilot projects for a variety of disciplines at schools in such states as Illinois, Indiana, Kentucky, Minnesota, Missouri, and Texas. Disciplines that Texas has been tuning include engineering, science, math, and business. In another exciting development, the American Historical Society has joined forces with Lumina to define what a degree in history should mean. Sixty institutions plan to use the results to tune their programs. The effort is being lead by historians at six institutions: Cleveland State, Colorado College, Georgia Tech, Raritan Valley Community College (NJ), University of California, San Diego, and Wheaton College (MA).

Until now, there haven't been any efforts to benchmark learning outcomes at the academic major level on a meaningful scale. These current efforts are significant because when schools define what students should be learning, it's much easier to then measure whether institutions are accomplishing what they promised to do.

Some Other Resources

While it's not easy locating learning outcomes for schools, you can find some useful information for more than 300 public universities and colleges by visiting the College Portrait of Undergraduate Education website (www.collegeportraits.org). College Portrait provides basic information about a school for a prospective student but also shares data from the National Survey of Student Engagement (NSSE).

While it doesn't measure learning outcomes, the NSSE surveys students in an attempt to assess how they are engaged on campuses in such areas as academic rigor, interactions with professors, and active and collaborative learning. Some schools hide their yearly results, but other institutions are happy to share them. You can learn more about the NSSE at its website (http://nsse.iub.edu/). An easy way to search for NSSE results is to head to the website of *USA Today*, which posts scores from cooperating schools. Here is the web address: http://www.usatoday.com/news/education/nsse.htm.

U-Can or University and College Accountability Network (www.ucan-network.org) is a similar consumer site for information on more than 800 private institutions that's sponsored by the National Association of Independent Colleges and Universities (NAIC). Unfortunately, the website doesn't provide any information about an institution's learning outcomes nor does it share NSEE results. A major reason why the NAIC isn't including this information is because the organization said that extensive research indicated that families weren't interested. How odd!

Finally, some of you might be wondering about the results of the CLA tests that provided those damning statistics for *Academically Adrift*. Some schools require their students to take the CLA, but many don't reveal the results because it would embarrass the institution. I was talking to the dean of social sciences at a prestigious research university once, and he said he planned to use the test to brag about his program until he looked at the scores and decided to bury the results instead. You can and should ask a school whether it uses the CLA and will share the results.

Action Plan

Measuring the quality of a school's academic offerings is in its infancy, but you should try to assess the commitment that an institution has shown in improving the educational experience of its undergraduates.

37

What's Wrong with *US News & World Report*'s College Rankings

When US News *asks a university president to perform the impossible task of assessing the relative merits of dozens of institutions he knows nothing about, he relies on the only source of detailed information at his disposal that assesses the relative merits of dozens of institutions that he knows nothing about:* US News.

—Malcolm Gladwell, *The New Yorker*

One summer, Baylor University contacted the freshman members of the graduating class of 2012 with an extremely odd request.

Baylor asked the students to retake the SAT. Now mind you, these students had long ago finished the admission process. They had put down their enrollment deposits and would arrive at the private Baptist university in the fall. Some may have already gone shopping for their dorm stuff.

Baylor, however, was offering the freshmen a $300 credit at the campus bookstore if they retook the SAT. Those who raised their scores by at least 50 points would receive a $1,000-a-year merit scholarship. Among those contacted, 861 students retook the SAT, and 150 of them pocketed the scholarships.

Why did Baylor bribe its freshmen into retaking a meaningless SAT exam? The Texas university's motivation can be summed up in two words: college rankings.

At the time, one of Baylor's institutional goals was to improve its status in *US News & World Report*'s college rankings. In fact, it wasn't a secret that the school was eager to propel itself to a spot among the top 50 universities. Higher standardized test scores is considered one way for a college to inch up in the popular rankings. Baylor's stunt, which provoked a huge outcry when it eventually hit the press, managed to boost the school's average SAT score by 10 points.

Baylor is hardly the only school that has fudged, or in some cases, falsified its numbers. A top administrator at Claremont McKenna College, for instance, was sent packing after the highly ranked liberal arts college discovered that for years he had inflated SAT test scores that were sent to *US News*. The US Naval Academy was embarrassed when it became public that its applicant rejection rate wasn't nearly as high as the institution reported. At an industry conference, a Clemson University administrator shared a laundry list of ways that her institution was manipulating its figures to boost its rankings, which included evaluating all other schools on *US News'* survey as below average.

College Rankings' Collateral Damage

Schools deservedly receive bad publicity when they are caught massaging or falsifying figures that are fed into the rankings algorithms, but what is infinitely more damaging is this: In the pursuit of rankings glory, schools across the country have adopted policies about how they spend their money, whom they admit, and what kind of financial aid they distribute that have negatively impacted millions of American families.

Even families that don't buy *US News'* annual best college guide (and they represent the vast majority of households with college-bound teenagers) are impacted by the rankings competition because of the actions of the audience that cares most deeply about the numbers. College presidents and their boards of trustees, and by extension their admission offices, are most transfixed by the rankings. *US News* has provided board members with an easy (though deeply flawed) scorecard to measure how their institutions are faring, and they are displeased if their school's ranking stalls out, or worse, drops.

Perhaps aggressive pursuit of higher rankings wouldn't be a bad thing if the rankings actually measured what sort of job an institution was doing to educate its undergraduates. One of the perverse aspects about the rankings is that turning out thoughtful, articulate young men and women who can write cogently and think critically isn't going to budge a school's ranking even one spot. Curiously enough, *US News* doesn't even attempt to measure the type of learning going on at schools.

Unfortunately, the methodology fueling the rankings is a collection of subjective measurements that students and families are supposed to rely upon to pinpoint the schools doing the best job of educating undergraduates. *US News* relies on proxies for educational quality, but as you'll learn these proxies are dubious at best.

A High Stakes Beauty Contest

While *US News* enjoys millions of hits on its website when it releases its annual rankings, few families appreciate how these numbers are compiled. How does one school get anointed No. 1, while others are relegated to the 29th, 53rd, or 194th spot?

To understand the impact that rankings have on higher-education practices, you need to appreciate how they are formulated. While *US News* wouldn't admit this, its rankings simply measure how prestigious, elite, and wealthy an institution is.

The biggest factor influencing the rankings is an institution's reputational score. Each year *US News* (I can't call it a magazine because it died, but the rankings machine lives on to grade such things as graduate schools, hospitals, doctors, cars, nursing homes, and diets!) dispatches three surveys to each school. Administrators in the offices of the president, provost, and admissions are supposed to complete the scorecards. Schools must grade their peers on a one-to-five scale, with five being the best.

The task is daunting for many reasons including the size of the peer groups. I counted 268 institutions in the national university category, including such disparate institutions as Brown, Yeshiva, Kent State, Texas Christian, Emory, Johns Hopkins, Virginia Tech, Dartmouth, Ball State, and Carnegie Mellon. What could the provost or president at Vanderbilt or the University of Connecticut possibly know about the academic quality of Hofstra University and the University of Oregon, as well as all the other schools that *US News* lumped together in this category? If this sounds crazy, I swear I'm not making this up!

The same scoring is used for the other peer groups, including the second prestige category—national liberal arts colleges. The folks at Amherst, Pomona, and Whitman colleges are supposed to know what's happening at Luther, Earlham, and Sweet Briar colleges and vice versa. Also nuts.

In an apparent effort to reduce the considerable flak it's received for its reputational beauty contest, which makes up 22.5% to 25% of a school's overall score, *US News* also includes the opinion of some high school counselors. Counselors, however, aren't going to be in any better position to measure the jobs individual schools are doing. (See Chapter 44, "What You Need to Know About High School Counselors.")

Malcolm Gladwell, who wrote a fascinating article about college rankings in *The New Yorker*, used an incident involving a former Michigan Supreme Court chief justice to illustrate the danger of basing scores on reputations. Years ago, the justice sent a questionnaire to about 100 lawyers and asked them to rank in order of quality ten law schools that included some Ivy League schools, as well as lesser-known institutions. As the judge recalled, Penn State's law school came in about in the middle. At the time, however, Penn State didn't even have a law school! (To find Gladwell's article, Google "What College Rankings Really Tell Us.")

Faced with an impossibly ludicrous task, administrators stuck with completing the survey will turn to *US News'* past college rankings to assess which schools are exceptional and which ones are simply ordinary. So previous reputations end up reinforcing future reputations. In other words, the rankings are a self-fulfilling prophecy.

US News' methodology favors well-known, elite schools even further by giving weight to the size of a school's endowment and the percentage of graduates who contribute to their alma mater. That's one of the reasons that you'll find few public universities in the higher rungs. Only three state institutions are among the top 25 universities—University of California, Berkeley, UCLA, and the University of Virginia.

College Rankings Hazards

Many teenagers end up as collateral damage in the rankings race because schools that are more selective are rated higher, which encourages them to accept more wealthy students. *US News* rewards schools that admit students with higher test scores and grade point averages. This focus on selectivity is a boon for affluent high school students, who tend to enjoy better academic profiles. These teens can afford expensive test-prep courses and are more likely to have attended college-prep schools with Advanced Placement and International Baccalaureate offerings. There is a strong correlation between standardized test scores and family income. The higher the parents' income, the higher the test scores are.

Before the rankings became so prominent, rich students typically had to pay full price for college. The majority of grants were reserved for middle-class and low-income students, who required financial help. But with the rankings premium linked to top students, public and private institutions began offering merit scholarships to entice smart, wealthy students to their campuses rather than to their competitors. How do you cough up the money for these deal sweeteners? One way is to raise the tuition to generate extra revenue for these scholarships, and another way is to reduce need-based financial aid.

The only schools that don't offer merit scholarships to rich students are perched at the top of the rankings heap. Wealthy parents whose children get into a Harvard or Swarthmore will be happy to write checks worth a quarter of a million dollars or more. The most elite schools boast that they reserve their aid for the families who need financial help to attend, but many of these institutions offer admission to a shamefully low percentage of needy students.

US News' algorithm also favors schools that spurn more students. To increase their rejection rates, some schools court students—through marketing materials and social media—that they have no intention of accepting. Here's another trick: Some institutions make it easy for students to apply via streamlined online applications, referred to in the industry as "fast apps." Schools use this strategy to increase the size of their student body, as well as bump up their rejection rates.

According to an article in *The Chronicle of Higher Education*, Drexel University, for instance, has been sending VIP applications to everyone in its inquiry pool. Teenagers are often flattered by these overtures and assume that their college suitors sincerely want them. They don't realize that the schools are enticing many students to apply so they can reject higher numbers. Ursinus College outside Philadelphia made *The New York Times* in 2011 when it abandoned its fast applications, but I doubt that many institutions have followed suit.

US News also places 20% of its grade on faculty resources, which includes professor salaries. No one, however, has shown a connection between what professors are paid and the quality of their teaching. In fact, the best-paid professors are often celebrated researchers who don't teach undergrads at all.

Another 10% of the grade is linked to a school's expenditures per student. The spending criterion has surely contributed to the frenetic pace of construction activity on campuses over the years. Because *US News* rewards institutions that spend tons of money, schools have little motivation to make their institutions more affordable.

Sadly, what the rankings giant ignores is how much debt students are incurring. It's a tragic omission that is certainly one reason why college tuition continues to defy inflation. Schools can spend freely and continue to raise tuition without worrying about getting hammered in the rankings. Of course, this behavior hurts families who are struggling to pay for the college experience.

Action Plan

You need to appreciate that *US News'* college rankings do not attempt to measure the type of education a student will receive at an institution. The rankings measure how elite and wealthy a school is.

38

The Right Way to Use College Rankings

As long as companies can publish magazines and students can choose colleges, someone will create college rankings that people will read and care about.

—Kevin Carey, policy director at Education Sector

If you've ever asked a teenager to name his or her dream schools, I bet these are some of the institutions that would pop up on the list:

- Stanford University
- Harvard University
- New York University
- Princeton University
- Massachusetts Institute of Technology
- Yale University
- UCLA
- University of Pennsylvania
- University of Southern California
- University of California, Berkeley

I actually copied those names from the Princeton Review's list of teenagers' most popular dream schools. The parents' list included many of the same universities, as well as Notre Dame, Duke, and Northwestern.

It's easy to see why Ivy League schools made the list because rightly or wrongly they are perceived to be the best. Despite its lousy financial aid awards, NYU is an extremely popular pick because, hey, look where it's located. How fun would it be to spend your college years roaming Manhattan? And as a Californian, I get why teenagers would like to attend the West Coast's most famous universities.

Do you, however, find anything troubling about these lists? I do because they show a serious lack of imagination among teenagers and their parents when it comes to generating ideas. For starters, all the Princeton Review schools are universities. Not a single college made the list. The teenagers also ignored any school that wasn't located on the East or West coasts.

Just like their parents, teenagers fall in love with name brands. They think certain schools are cool because millions of other teenagers have thought the same thing.

The typical college dream list, however, doesn't serve students well. The popularity of these dreams schools makes them nearly impossible to penetrate. Just check out these rejection rates: USC (77%), Northwestern (77%), UC Berkeley (78%), Penn (88%), and Yale (92%). These rejection rates, by the way, are outliers. According to the College Board, only 2% of schools reject 75% or more of their applicants.

As a practical matter, the majority of students may dream of going to USC or NYU, but most end up attending public colleges and universities within a two-hour drive of their homes. Many of them never seriously explore any realistic alternatives. That's a shame because there are wonderful schools scattered across the country if teenagers and their families would just cast a wider net.

Students could end up with a richer assortment of schools if they used the rankings intelligently. The best way to use rankings, whether they are from *US News*, *Forbes*, *Washington Monthly*, or the *Princeton Review* is to use them as tip sheets. If you spend time with these lists, you will be able to seriously consider a larger circle of promising candidates.

Looking at College Rankings

An obvious starting point for gathering names is *US News'* college rankings. Look at these rankings with this caveat: Please don't assume that the No. 1 school must be better than school No. 2, No. 50, or the school ranked as 100th best. It's up to you to evaluate what schools are best for you. Don't be a slave to meaningless numbers.

US News has four categories of schools:

- National universities
- National liberal arts colleges
- Regional universities
- Regional colleges

The national university category hogs the most attention because this is the turf where Harvard, Princeton, and Yale wrestle for the No. 1 title. You are probably going to be more familiar with these schools because they include the nation's flagship institutions and prominent private universities.

The institutions in the other three categories are more likely to contain schools that you've never heard about. For example, the top 100 schools in the liberal arts category include such names as Allegheny College (Pennsylvania), Illinois Wesleyan University, Kalamazoo College (Michigan), Sewanee-University of the South (Tennessee), Southwestern University (Texas), University of Puget Sound (Washington), and Willamette University (Oregon).

You'll also find well-regarded schools in the regional university category that you probably didn't know existed such as Bentley University (Massachusetts), Bradley University (Illinois), College of Charleston (South Carolina), Elon University (North Carolina), Marist College (New York), Otterbein College (Ohio), Rollins College (Florida), and Trinity University (Texas).

And it's the same story in the regional college category with such names as Carroll College (Montana), Cooper Union (New York),

Elizabethtown College (Pennsylvania), Elmira College (New York), High Point University (North Carolina), Marietta College (Ohio), and Taylor University (Indiana).

Once you've gathered names, it's up to you to start researching schools to see which could turn into promising prospects.

Action Plan

Don't rely on somebody else's dream school list; research schools and develop your own. Doing the research yourself should lead to a better collection of schools.

39

College Rankings: An Alternative

Does much learning occur at the University of Michigan, Colorado College, or the University of Texas at San Antonio? Do students at Duke University fare better in the job market than their counterparts at Northwestern or Cornell? There are so many important questions like these regarding higher education for which we do not have answers, and colleges have generally resisted providing that information in a uniform manner that would allow comparisons of performance at colleges and universities by consumers, funders, and taxpayers generally.

—Richard Vedder, economics professor at Ohio University and director of the Center for College Affordability and Productivity

While *US News & World Report's* college rankings monopolize the attention, I much prefer *Forbes* magazine's rankings.

Forbes' rankings are imperfect (all rankings are), but they represent a significant improvement over *US News'* scorecards because the magazine takes a stab at addressing what kind of return on investment students and their parents can expect from schools.

Forbes' rankings aim to measure the sort of educational experience that students are receiving, as well as their success in obtaining jobs after graduation. *Forbes* also evaluates schools based on how much debt their students must grapple with after graduation. Strangely enough, *US News* doesn't use any of these measures.

The *Forbes* rankings measure these five areas:

- Student satisfaction (A big factor is RateMyProfessor.com evaluations.)
- Postgraduate success (Graduates' salaries compiled by PayScale.com.)
- Student debt (How much students owe upon graduation.)
- Four-year grad rate (Most students don't graduate in four years.)
- Student competitive awards (Includes Rhodes, Fulbright, Watson, and more.)

The Center for College Affordability and Productivity, an education think tank, developed the methodology for the *Forbes* rankings and has been producing the annual lists since they were rolled out in 2008. You can find a lengthy explanation of the magazine's methodology, which continues to evolve, at the think tank's website (http:// centerforcollegeaffordability.org/). On the home page, just click on the Rankings tab.

While you can head to the magazine's website to check out the rankings, I prefer to look on the center's website for the lists that are sliced and diced in a variety of ways. You'll see the master list of the 650 college and universities that are ranked in order, as well as lists of the institutions broken down in a variety of other ways including by geographic region. You might find the rankings by region particularly helpful since most students don't stray too far from home. It's my opinion that far more students could be attending schools in distant ZIP codes, but often parents and teenagers aren't sure where to look.

Forbes College Rankings Results

Some darlings of *US News'* rankings, such as Williams, Amherst, Stanford, Harvard, and the University of Chicago, also rise to the top of *Forbes'* rankings, but other big names dropped. Prestigious schools that didn't crack the top 50 schools in *Forbes'* list include Cornell, Johns Hopkins, University of Pennsylvania, New York University,

University of Southern California, University of Michigan, and Washington University in St. Louis.

In contrast, schools that fared better in the rankings than some of those heavy hitters include such institutions as Centre College (Kentucky), St. Michael's College (Vermont), Transylvania University (Kentucky), St. Norbert College (Wisconsin), Hillsdale College (Michigan), Knox College (Illinois), St. Olaf College (Minnesota), Hobart and William Smith Colleges (New York), and the University of Minnesota at Morris, a public liberal arts college that gives in-state tuition to all students! The school in Morris edged out the University of Michigan at Ann Arbor.

Am I suggesting that schools like St. Anselm College and Furman University are superior to UCS and Carnegie Mellon University because they fared better in the rankings? No. These are different kinds of institutions and each possesses its own strengths and weaknesses. What I am strongly suggesting is that people should begin the college search without harboring preconceived notions about which schools are superior and which aren't.

Action Plan

Don't get hung up on the specific college rankings and instead use the lists as tip sheets to generate names of schools that ideally will open up your search to a much wider universe.

40

The Hallmarks of a Student-Centered University

Higher education has lost track of its original and endur-
ing purpose: to challenge the minds and imaginations of this
nation's young people, to expand their understanding of the
world, and thus themselves.

—Andrew Hacker and Claudia Dreifus, *Higher Education?*
How Colleges Are Wasting Our Money and Failing Our
Kids—And What We Can Do About It

What should you learn in college?

In higher-ed circles, you can find academics who believe specific disciplinary content is king. English majors, for instance, should have certain concepts, dates, and facts lodged inside their cranium before they graduate. I assume that would mean Beowulf, John Donne poems, Shakespeare, and a bunch of stuff found in a well-thumbed copy of the *Norton Anthology of English Literature.*

Rather than focusing just on content, a growing number of educators believe that institutions best serve their students by also making sure that they help students develop core skills such as thinking critically and writing persuasively. They would agree that an English major should get acquainted with Chaucer and *The Iliad* before graduating, but they are more concerned that the academic experiences for students are fashioned in a way that they will benefit long after they forget why Beowulf is important. In higher-ed circles, the advocates of constructing college curriculum and experiences for students with core skills in mind are clearly winning the day.

Portland State University is one institution that has embraced the core skills approach to learning. All of Portland State's students attend classes through either an honors path or the University Studies program where they attend interdisciplinary seminars designed to develop those important core skills such as writing, collaborating, and taking an active part in learning. This sort of arrangement is infinitely better than the passive experience many university students experience when they sit in the lecture hall while a professor yammers away on the stage.

Portland State, which has been highly lauded nationally for its efforts, is not the sort of campus where you'd expect to find cutting-edge innovation. Portland State, to be sure, faces challenges. A third of the students at the commuter school are low-income, an even greater number are part-time, and nearly four in ten are past the traditional college age. The institution's graduation rate is low. This urban institution, however, has been working far harder than many of its prestigious peers to make the education of its students meaningful.

Another way that schools are working to engage undergraduates is by disrupting the traditional lecture-hall style learning. Some professors, for instance, are taping their lectures and requiring students to listen to them in advance. This frees up class time for interactive exercises. Other teachers are directing their students to self-paced computer courses and using the traditional lecture time to answer questions.

Collegiate Best Practices

The experience of Portland State and other schools illustrates that you can't just look at college rankings and know whether schools are dedicated to providing their undergraduates with a quality education. But how do you find universities and colleges that are truly serious about educating undergrads?

Here's one suggestion: look for schools that have shown a commitment to supporting high-impact practices that research suggests increase a student's likelihood of succeeding. The Association of

American Colleges and Universities has compiled a list of these best practices that are based on much research.

The following ten practices have a nearly universal positive impact on students because they lead to more student and faculty interaction and higher levels of student engagement, which increases the chances of students ultimately graduating.

Learning communities. Some universities are helping students successfully transition from high school by grouping them into learning communities. Schools can establish learning communities in a variety of ways. Some universities schedule groups of students, who are often freshmen, to enroll in two or more courses together. The students may take some type of freshman seminar together, as well as other classes. When the classes are linked by an interdisciplinary theme, the professors often collaborate. At some schools, the students also live in the same dorms. Some universities call their learning communities Freshmen or First-Year Interest Groups (FIGs).

Studies from the National Survey of Student Engagement, a non-profit group based at Indiana University that promotes student learning, show that students in learning communities become far more engaged in college than those without the experience. These students talk more with professors and their classmates. The students not only studied more, but did so in a more meaningful way.

You can find hundreds of schools with learning communities by visiting the website of the Washington Center for Improving the Quality of Undergraduate Education, housed at Evergreen State College in Olympia, Washington (www.evergreen.edu/washcenter/home.asp).

First-year seminars and experiences. Some of these first-year experiences are extended orientation seminars, while others are academic or study skill seminars. You can find some of the institutions with freshman experiences at the website of the National Resource Center, First-Year Experience and Students in Transition at the University of South Carolina. Just Google the name.

Common intellectual experiences. Much as Portland State has done, schools go beyond the core curriculum to cultivate core skills in students that can be achieved through interdisciplinary themes.

Writing-intensive courses. Ideally schools will require writing across the curriculum and not just in disciplines like English and philosophy. At many universities, writing gets short shrift because grading papers is labor intensive. When employers are surveyed about what they are looking for in employees, however, writing ability is high on their wish lists.

Collaborative assignments and projects. Students, suggests the association, are more apt to succeed at a school that requires students to collaborate. Approaches range from study groups within courses to team-based assignments and writing to cooperative projects and research.

Undergraduate research. Graduate students enjoy most of the research opportunities, but there are institutions where undergrads also get a chance. Students can benefit by working closely with a faculty mentor and the experience can also give them a boost getting into graduate school.

Diversity/global learning. Some schools are emphasizing courses and programs that help students explore cultures, life experiences, and worldviews different from their own. Frequently these intercultural studies are augmented by experiential learning in the nearby community and/or by studying abroad.

Internships. Graduates who have had meaningful internships can enjoy an advantage over their peers in the job market.

Service learning, community-based learning. In some classes, students experience experiential learning with community partners. A key element to these classes is to apply what they've learned in real-world settings and reflect in the classroom on what they've learned.

Capstone courses and projects. Also look for universities that offer capstone projects for seniors. A capstone project requires students to apply what they have learned in their major field of study in a project that allows them to demonstrate a mastery of the curriculum.

Action Plan

Look for colleges and universities that make student-centered undergraduate education a priority.

41

Staying in College Too Long

Time is the enemy of college completion.

—Report from Complete College America, a nonprofit

A mom once told me that she made her son, who was heading off to San Jose State University in the fall, promise that he would graduate in four years. No fooling around, she insisted.

The mother looked stunned, however, when I told her that it was highly unlikely that her child, regardless of his promise, would graduate on time. San Jose State's four-year grad rate is just 7.7%.

San Jose State may be an extreme case, but most students who are attending college right now will not be graduating in four years. Many find it tough to make it within six years. In that period of time, just 58% cross the finish line.

I have yet to meet any parents who want their children's college graduation ceremony delayed by a year or two. Not only does that extra schooling make the price of a diploma more expensive, but there's also the lost opportunity cost. When students can't graduate on time, they aren't getting a start on their careers.

There's been little outcry among families about dismal college graduation rates, but it's understandable. If parents and teenagers don't know that rates are low—and most schools are loathe to publicize them—they aren't going to complain.

The nation's noncompetitive schools, which the bulk of college students attend, obviously drag down the national graduation rates. For instance, less than 1% of students at Mountain State University in Beckley, West Virginia, which accepts all applicants, graduate in four years. In comparison, 93% of Williams College undergrads earn their diploma by then.

Obviously the types of students that Williams and Mountain State attract aren't crossing paths. What's important, however, is that a surprising variation in graduation rates exists between colleges and universities with similar admission standards and student bodies. If your child is aiming for selective private liberal arts colleges, for instance, you'll want to compare schools that belong in this category. If you are looking at regional public universities in your state, compare that group.

As a general rule, students at private colleges and universities graduate sooner than their peers attending state institutions. Not surprisingly, among state institutions, flagships, which tend to attract better-prepared students and also enjoy greater resources, produce the highest grad rates. Among private schools, intensive research universities, which would include schools like the Ivies, Georgetown, MIT, Duke, University of Chicago, and Stanford, enjoy the highest grad rates, followed by liberal arts colleges. The public and private universities where the highest degree you can attain is typically a master's degree sport the lowest rates.

College Results Online

Luckily, graduation track records are easy to obtain to help you evaluate the job a college or university is doing. When you are evaluating schools, you should always obtain their graduation rates.

The simplest way to find a school's grad rate is to use the tool at The Education Trust's College Results Online (www.collegeresults. org). Type in the name of any school on the home page, and you'll find its four-, five-, and six-year graduation rates.

Once you've retrieved the stats for a school, you should then compare them with peer institutions. Luckily, College Results Online makes this part simple. When you're looking at the grad rate of a school, you will see a Similar Colleges tab near the top of the page. Click on it to obtain a list of that school's peer institutions along with the six-year grad rates for each of them. The six-year rate is the default setting, but you can change it to four years by using the pull-down menu marked Grad Rate Timeframe and updating the table.

A Flagship University's Grad Rate

I'm using the University of Illinois at Urbana-Champaign to illustrate what you can find on College Results Online. On the site, I discovered that Illinois' four-year grad rate is nearly 65%, which is high for a public research university. When I clicked on the Similar Colleges link, a table instantly appeared that included such Illini peers as the University of Michigan, University of Maryland, Penn State, Ohio State, University of Florida, University of Wisconsin, and University of Texas.

The chart showed that Illinois was second among 15 peer schools, which were predominantly flagships. University of Michigan enjoyed the highest grad rate of 72.7%, and North Carolina State and University of Colorado sported the lowest rates at 41.6% and 41.1%, respectively. That's obviously a huge spread. You can also expand the field by directing the software to produce 25 peer institutions and sometimes even 50 if there are that many comparable institutions.

Grad Rates at Private Colleges

Using the tool, you can discover promising schools that you didn't know existed or become more cautious about others. Every search can generate something unexpected. That was true when I took a look at Lafayette College, a highly regarded liberal arts college in Pennsylvania. Among 15 peer institutions, Lafayette's four-year grad rate (86%) was excellent. Only Bucknell University and the College of the Holy Cross fared better at 87.6% and 87%, respectively. Lafayette remained in the same position when I expanded the list to 25 comparable schools.

Lafayette's highly selective peers included St. Olaf College, Smith College, Colorado College, Kalamazoo College, Occidental College, Dickinson College, and Rhodes College, a beautiful school in Memphis that graces the cover of this book. The four-year grad rates for these schools were fairly close, but there were some exceptions. The schools sitting at the bottom were Hampshire College (54.8%) and Bennington College (48.8%).

Coincidentally, I was talking with a young woman recently whose No. 1 college choice is Hampshire. She visited the Massachusetts school and was impressed by its programs, as well as the students and professors she met. She was unaware, however, of the low graduation rate for this school that costs more than $55,000 a year. I suggested that she find out why the grad rate for her favorite school is low before she finalized her plans.

How Happy Are the Freshmen?

Actually, I already knew one of the one reasons for Hampshire's poor showing compared to its peers. Fewer freshmen appear to be happy at Hampshire. How do I know that? I checked the school's freshman retention rate, which is the percentage of first-year students who return for their sophomore year.

The freshman retention rate for both Hampshire and Bennington colleges was 79%. In comparison, Lafayette's freshman retention rate was 94%. You can find freshman retention rates for any school at College Results Online.

If you're wondering what average freshman retention rates are nationally, ACT, Inc., the test maker, keeps tabs. When two- and four-year institutions are lumped together, the average freshman retention rate is just 67%. The average retention rate for four-year schools is nearly 73%. The more exclusive a school is, typically the more impressive its retention rate. To find the latest annual ACT report, Google its title: "National Collegiate Retention and Persistence to Degree Rates."

How Graduation Rates Are Calculated

Unhappy freshmen can deflate a school's grad rate because of the strange and controversial way that the U.S. Department of Education generates statistics. (College Results Online obtains its grad rates from the federal government.) The federal government only keeps tabs of students who are full-time freshmen when they start college. Students who begin college part-time have never been included in the official grad rates. That omission ignores a huge swath of students. Four out of ten students attending public institutions, for instance, are part-timers.

The federal government also doesn't track students who transfer from one four-year school to another. The federal data system essentially treats these students as college dropouts even though many graduate from other schools. Consequently, when a significant number of students leave a school, such as at Bennington and Hampshire, the grad rates at these colleges take a hit simply because of the exodus. No one tracks these departing students to see whether they ever graduate elsewhere. Instead they are counted as students who failed to graduate from their original schools. That's one reason why it's just about impossible for even the most elite schools to get close to a 100% graduation rate.

The federal government is under pressure to change the grad rate methodology. Complete College America, an endeavor supported by the Bill & Melinda Gates Foundation and other foundations, is one of the big proponents of more meaningful graduation figures. The backers of Complete College America believe that until graduation data is available for *all* college students, it will be difficult to know what works and what doesn't in terms of getting students to the finish line. Without this data, it will also be hard to reward schools that excel or to hold failing schools accountable.

Public Institutions with the Highest Four-Year Grad Rates

1. U.S. Naval Academy: 88.2%
2. University of Virginia: 84.4%
3. College of William and Mary: 83.2%

4. U.S. Military Academy: 79.7%

5. U.S. Coast Guard Academy: 79.1%

6. U.S. Air Force Academy: 77.0%

7. College of New Jersey: 72.7%

8. University of Michigan: 72.7%

9. University of North Carolina: 72.2%

10. St. Mary's College of Maryland: 71.3%

11. Miami University-Oxford, Ohio: 70.5%

12. United States Merchant Marine Academy: 68.5%

13. UCLA: 67.2%

14. University of Mary Washington: 67.1%

15. The Citadel: 67.0%

Private Institutions with the Highest Four-Year Grad Rates

1. Williams College: 93.2%

2. Yale University: 90.4%

3. University of Notre Dame: 90.1%

4. Princeton University: 89.9%

5. Carleton College and Soka University of America: 89.1%

6. Davidson College and Franklin W. Olin College of Engineering: 89.0%

7. Pomona College: 88.9%

8. Bowdoin College: 88.8%

9. Babson College, Duke University, and Wesleyan University: 88.5%

10. Boston College: 88.0%

11. Haverford College: 87.9%

12. Harvard, Georgetown, Washington & Lee, and Vassar: 87.8%

13. University of Pennsylvania and Bucknell University: 87.6%

14. Northwestern University: 87.3%

15. College of the Holy Cross: 87.0%

The Graduation Disadvantage

Comparing grad rates of schools is important, but I'd urge you to dig deeper. College Results Online also allows you to check grad rates by race, ethnicity, and gender.

You can check, for instance, to see how many men versus women graduate from individual schools. At most colleges and universities, women graduate at higher rates. Among the 25 private colleges and universities with the highest four-year grad rates, women enjoyed better grad rates at 22 of the schools and sometimes by a wide margin. At Northwestern University, for instance, 91% of women versus 83% of men graduated in the traditional eight semesters. At Yale, 94% of women versus 87% of men graduated on time.

You can also use College Results Online to check the graduation breakdown at individual schools for students who are Asian, African American, Latino, Native American, and white. Clearly, students of any race want to attend schools where most students successfully graduate, but at some institutions there is a gulf between grad rates of white students and minorities.

Schools that are making a concerted effort to close the graduation gap between white classmates and minorities will benefit all students because that means they are instituting changes that will enhance the educational experience for everyone.

Action Plan

When researching schools, always check their four-year graduation rates. Use College Results Online to generate lists of potential schools.

42

Grading Academic Departments

> One of the most common questions I am asked is, "What are the best colleges for my intended major?" I've been asked this by prospective majors in just about every subject imaginable. My reply is always the same: You are asking the wrong question. The real question students and parents should be asking at the start of their college search is not which programs are "best," but rather "what are the elements of a strong program in a particular major?"

—Carolyn Z. Lawrence, private college counselor

When *US News & World Report* declared in the mid 2000s that the economics department at the University of California, San Diego, had earned its way onto the list of the nation's top ten econ departments, it was considered a coup.

UCSD, a highly respected research institution that had only been around since 1960, was joining such august company as Harvard University, Massachusetts Institute of Technology, and Stanford University. *US News & World Report* was hardly the only entity tossing bouquets at the economics department that had two Nobel Prize winners on its faculty.

Lost in the celebration, however, was the kind of experience that undergraduate economics majors were having at this prestigious campus. The econ department's stellar reputation had been attracting a growing number of students over the years, but the staffing wasn't keeping up with the enrollment.

An article in the *San Diego Union-Tribune* in 2006 touched on the difficulties that the undergrads faced. Eleven years earlier, 837 undergraduates were in the economics department, but the number had swelled to 1,900. The department, however, wasn't much bigger. At the time the story was written, the department had 32 full-time professors, which was only five more than in 1995. Comparable economics departments, the article noted, typically employed 15 more faculty members and had fewer students to teach. What's more, temporary lecturers were teaching a quarter of UCSD's econ classes.

An honors student quoted in the newspaper story said that she and other students had complained about large class sizes and their lack of access to the vaunted faculty. In fact, some upper-division economics classes, where you'd expect to have smaller numbers, were crammed with up to 150 students.

What astounded me when I read the article was that the department had the ability to hire more econ professors, but had failed to do so. Why? The department chair explained that while the nation was producing about 1,000 new PhDs a year, the department only considered about 50 of them to be of a high enough caliber to pursue. "We couldn't find 15 people that (a) we wanted and (b) would come," the chair explained. Tough luck for those UCSD undergrads! By the way, I recently ran into a UCSD senior who is majoring in economics, and he told me that the large class sizes for upperclassmen remain the same.

Why do I mention UCSD's sweet and sour record? Because reputations can be deceiving. UCSD, like so many other highly ranked universities, receives accolades because of its cutting-edge research, not because of the attention it pays to its undergraduates. Will it matter to undergrads if some professors are Nobel laureates if their only contact with them is waving from the 20th row of a lecture hall? Maybe it will and maybe it won't, but I think students will benefit from knowing what they can expect.

When researching a school, look beyond its reputation to see how the institution treats its undergraduates. You can begin by looking at the experience that students in your expected major are having.

Action Plan

Do your due diligence and find out how the undergraduates are being treated at schools on your list.

43

Kicking the Tires

> The technological sophistication required to satisfy questions about student learning and educational gains does not yet exist. Asking tougher questions about student learning ensures that we know much more than we did a generation ago. This also means we are learning how much we don't know about student learning.
>
> —James T. Minor, director of higher education programs at Southern Education Foundation

Here are a few final suggestions on how you can get a sense about the academic quality at a college or university.

Visit RateMyProfessor.com. Check out how students have sized up their teachers at RateMyProfessors.com. While there is a debate about the validity of this measurement of teacher quality, The Center for College Affordability and Productivity, a higher-ed think tank, believes in its validity enough to use the scores as a factor in the college rankings it produces annually for *Forbes* magazine.

I looked at the ratings of a few of my children's college professors and the scores seemed in line with what they experienced in the classroom. In addition to individual professor ratings, you can check out a school's composite faculty score on a five-point scale. When I checked the composite faculty scores for two Ivy League institutions—Yale University (2.59) and Columbia University (2.37)—I wasn't surprised to see poor numbers because intensive research institutions aren't known for their teaching. Colleges are much more likely to seek out professors who are great teachers. In contrast to the two Ivies, here are two prestigious colleges—Amherst College (3.8) and Harvey Mudd (3.77)—that enjoy excellent overall professor ratings.

Look for a commitment to academic excellence. Plenty of professors get stuck in a rut. They teach the same way, year in and year out, as their material becomes drier than burnt toast. Some of these educators would rather cling to the familiar than explore new approaches.

This pigheadedness is what educators who participated in an online discussion hosted by *The Chronicle of Higher Education* grumbled about one morning. The professors, scattered around the country, had gathered on the web to hear the thoughts of Robert J. Beichner, a physics professor at North Carolina State University in Raleigh. Beichner has received kudos for developing a promising way to banish impersonal lectures for science and engineering students. Schools throughout the country, including the Massachusetts Institute of Technology, have adopted the teaching approach.

In talking about the academic resistance to change, Beichner shared his take on the phenomenon: "It's probably true that nearly all higher education faculty members were very good students in the traditional classroom setting. This leads to inertia. 'It was good enough for me, so it's good enough for them.' So many introductory courses become filters instead of pumps. What ends up happening is that people who think as we do will succeed and the rest won't. But we can no longer afford to only concentrate ourselves with 2% or 3% of our students."

Creative teaching approaches are especially important early on because that's when students are likely to wash out. Large impersonal lecture classes can prompt students to lose interest or abandon grueling majors.

There is no definitive source to find out about innovative teaching. If a department is committed to quality teaching for its undergraduates, however, it will probably tout its efforts on its website. When you contact professors by email or during a campus visit, ask about teaching approaches.

Check department websites. The online home of academic departments should provide a more unfiltered look at a commitment to undergraduate learning (if it exists) compared to the perennial upbeat messages emanating from the admission website.

When looking at a department's online home, pay attention to the kind of opportunities and experiences that undergrads have. Are there research and internships opportunities for undergrads? Will students have the ability to tackle a capstone project, which requires working with a professor? How big are the classes?

Ultimately, what you'd like to see is a department that's got plenty to brag about. The physics department at North Carolina State University in Raleigh, for example, is not shy about touting its accomplishments.

The department's faculty have won outstanding teaching awards and, as mentioned earlier, the department has instituted an innovative way of teaching introductory courses that's spread elsewhere. On its website, the department boasts that it combines the "resources of a major research university with the ambience of a small college." The department offers "small classes, personal attention, and unparalleled opportunities for involvement in research." It's impressive to see a department display this kind of enthusiasm, drive, and achievement.

Check the numbers. Statistics can be misleading. And a big whopper is often the student-to-faculty ratio, which you'll find in many college guides. To get that figure, schools divide the number of faculty into the number of students. There are a lot of ways to fudge this number, which makes it pretty much worthless. For instance, professors who rarely or never teach undergraduates are included in the count, and sometimes graduates student assistants are also treated as faculty.

For a more realistic alternative, ask about the average class size of courses at the school as well as introductory classes and those in your major.

Talk to students. This might seem obvious, but many prospective students never bother to direct questions to those already enrolled at the school.

Read the trades. You can learn a great deal about academic issues by peeking over the shoulders of journalists who cover the college world for *The Chronicle of Higher Education* and *Inside Higher Ed.*

Inside Higher Ed (www.insidehighered.com), a free online trade publication, provides daily news and commentary about academia. The better-known *Chronicle* (www.chronicle.com) publishes a print and online edition, but requires a subscription for many stories. Both publications archive their stories, which will make any search easier. It's simple to use these publications with their myriad of links to their own archives and to outside organizations as a cheap or free research assistant no matter what education topic you want to research.

Check out professional organizations. You can learn a lot about a particular major, the institutions that offer it, innovative teaching approaches, and potential careers by eavesdropping on what professionals and/or educators in a particular field are saying. Some professional organizations go out of their way to welcome students or prospective students in their fields.

One of the nice things about some of these professional groups is the low cost. A student, for example, can join the American Society for Engineering Educators for a nominal fee. In return, a student member receives an award-winning magazine that includes articles about educators and engineering program innovations.

Thanks to Google, it shouldn't be tough finding professional organizations tied to a student's possible major. You can also track these groups down through College Majors 101 (www.collegemajors101.com).

Look for student organizations. Many organizations exist that are devoted to students or prospective students in particular fields. A great place for wannabe architects, for example, is ARCHcareers.org, which is connected to the American Institute of Architecture Students (AIAS) and The American Institute of Architects. The site, which includes a blog, is dedicated to helping high school students and undergraduates who want to study architecture. College Majors 101 is also a source for finding student associations.

Keep abreast of college major changes. You might think that certain majors, such as computer science and engineering, are more prone to changes in curriculum content than others. Any major, however, can benefit from change. When researching academic majors at particular schools, it makes sense to discover whether they are participating in any leading-edge innovations.

Foreign language provides an example of this phenomenon. As with some other humanities departments, language teachers have been instructing students pretty much the same way for decades. Traditionally, students master a language's vocabulary and grammar rules and then they devote the rest of their time to taking advanced literature classes in the foreign language. The Modern Language Association, which is the professional organization for language teachers, now insists, however, that this age-old way of teaching is antiquated. Writing brilliant papers in French on *Madame Bovary* and *Candide* isn't necessarily going to prepare you for jobs that require bilingual skills. Consequently, language departments are being urged to introduce curriculums that can better prepare students for a global society. That means bringing in other disciplines that can better help them use their language proficiency in a variety of careers.

Since many of the professors in language departments are literature professors, some institutions haven't embraced the changes that the Modern Language Association has advocated. Learning about this innovation in language education, however, can help wannabe language majors to formulate more intelligent questions for department faculty. And language students will need to ask themselves if they want to learn the old-fashioned way or not.

Action Plan

When evaluating schools, don't just stop at its reputation or ranking. The tools are imperfect, but there are ways to kick the tires.

Part V

Admission Nuts and Bolts

44

What You Need to Know About High School Counselors

Most young people who go on to college believe that the advice of their high school counselors was inadequate and often impersonal and perfunctory. When asked about their experiences with their counselors in high school, about half say that they felt like "just another face in the crowd."

—Public Agenda study prepared for the Bill & Melinda Gates Foundation

I once volunteered to write an article for a newsletter published by the Western Association for College Admission Counseling (WACAC), a regional organization of high school guidance counselors, private college consultants, and college staff and administrators. I turned in an article about financial aid and forgot about it until I was notified that the newsletter committee had rejected my submission. Why?

The high school counselor, who was in charge of putting together the newsletter, explained that the committee didn't think that financial aid was an *appropriate* subject. The counselor explained that financial aid is never covered in the organization's newsletter and that high school counselors have to be careful because of *liability* issues. My submission, she told me, was the first article that the committee had ever rejected.

This incident would hardly be worth sharing except that I think it helps to illustrate a serious problem bedeviling the guidance counseling profession. High school counselors are not trained to understand financial aid issues. In fact, many counselors are so intimidated by the topic of financial aid and other college affordability issues that they try to avoid knowing any specifics about how parents are supposed to pay for college.

This lack of knowledge obviously has tremendous consequences for millions of families across the country who turn to their high school counselors for answers. With the price of college continuing to climb, families are arguably more desperate than ever to learn how to make college more affordable, but they usually aren't getting answers at their high schools.

It Goes Beyond the Numbers

When the media focuses on the state of high school counseling, it's often discussed in terms of workload. Counselors rightfully complain that the number of students they are expected to assist is ridiculously high. According to the American School Counselor Association, the optimum student-counselor ratio is 250 to 1. In California, however, the number is closer to 1,000 to 1. In such states as Minnesota, Utah, and Arizona, the ratio can be more than 700 to 1. Nationally, it's estimated that there is one counselor for every 459 high school students.

All the talk about high student-counselor ratios, however, has masked the equally troubling issue of ill-trained counselors. Even if the workloads of counselors miraculously dropped to reasonable levels, many counselors still wouldn't be able to provide meaningful college counseling to families because they don't know enough themselves.

If counselors were knowledgeable about college issues, they would be able to give schoolwide presentations to families on issues like financial aid, merit aid, and admission trends. They could explain how parents can determine which schools are generous and which aren't by turning to online tools. They could talk about the importance of using net price calculators and share how parents can obtain their Expected Family Contribution.

Getting this valuable information in a packed high school auditorium isn't as desirable as a counselor working one-on-one with families, but it would be far superior to what many students and their parents are experiencing today.

High student-counselors ratios should not be an excuse for counselors failing to understand the basics of college admission and financial aid.

Inadequate Counselor Education

Why aren't counselors being properly trained? Considerable blame can be dumped on the hundreds of graduate schools of education in this country. To work in public schools, most counselors must earn a master's degree in counseling through these graduate schools, but these programs rarely offer even a single class in college planning. Instead the coursework focuses on such issues as mental health and careers. Careers but not college planning? Really, I'm not making this up!

Counseling master's degree programs ignore college issues that high school counselors need to know. I'm not just talking about all the financial topics that families must face with their college-bound teenagers. They also don't touch on others issues of critical importance, such as evaluating colleges academically. If you asked many high school counselors what are the differences between a college and a university, I bet they'd be stumped.

Hidebound schools of education, which have deservedly received criticism for how they educate the nation's teachers, have resisted reevaluating their counselor curriculum. Trying to nudge these graduate schools into offering classes on critical issues for college-bound teenagers has been discouraging.

Bob Bardwell, a director of counseling at a public high school in Massachusetts, once told me about his experience on a task force of the National Association for College Admission Counseling (NACAC) that tried to encourage schools of education to add even a single college planning course into their curriculum. The effort, Bardwell lamented, was not successful. NACAC, by the way, is the mother organization for many regional groups including WACAC, which imposed that financial-aid-free zone for its newsletter.

Counselor Feedback

When you consider the lack of counselor training and their large caseloads, it's no surprise that counselors have not fared well in opinion polls.

Counselors, for instance, received poor scores in a Public Agenda survey that was underwritten by the Bill & Melinda Gates Foundation, a major player in education reform. In the survey, 67% of Americans ages 22 to 30 concluded that their high school counselors did a *fair* or *poor* job of helping them with their college choices, and 62% said they were equally disappointing in helping them explore potential careers.

The responses, according to the report's authors, "suggest that the existing high school guidance system is a perilously weak part of the nation's efforts to increase college attendance and ramp up degree completion. As the survey demonstrates, the judgments young people make about their high school counselors are often harsh, considerably harsher than the judgments they make about their high school teachers or their advisers at the postsecondary level."

What Colleges Think

Another recent nationwide study of more than 400 senior college admission officers by *Inside Higher Ed*, an online trade publication, was just as damning. The administrators were asked to rate the effectiveness of resources that students use in the college admission process. Public high school counselors didn't even crack the administrators' top five resources, which you can see here:

1. College counselors at private high schools
2. Financial aid/scholarship websites, such as FAFSA, FastWeb, and FinAid.org
3. Social media sources, such as College Confidential and Facebook
4. Independent/private college counselors
5. Data-driven college counseling tools, such as Naviance

The assessment of college administrators didn't surprise me. When I've talked with college admission deans on this subject, they confide privately that their opinion of public high school counselors is low. It's obviously a touchy subject for them, and they don't want to experience the wrath of counselors by airing their opinions out loud.

I want to emphasize that there are some tremendously bright and energetic public high school counselors in this country who understand the college process. I have met some of them, and they are inspiring. The best of them understand how to evaluate schools academically and financially. These counselors have often taken the time to educate themselves by reading books and doing research online. Counselors absolutely do not have to attend expensive conferences to become educated on college issues.

Counselors at Private High Schools

Are counselors at private high schools any better prepared? Generally yes.

As you just learned, respondents in the *Inside Higher Ed* survey agreed that the most effective resource for students in the college admission process are counselors at private high schools.

Private schools typically do not require counselors to have master's degrees, but as you've already learned, these degrees are useless in preparing the degree holders to help families with college choices.

Anecdotally, I can tell you that the counselors at private schools that I've encountered or heard about excel in expanding their students' universe of college possibilities. Most teenagers in the United States end up attending schools within 100 miles of their homes, but these colleges aren't always the best or most affordable options. Private counselors are more likely to know about colleges and universities throughout the country, which gives students at these high schools an advantage.

Admittedly, counselors at private high schools typically enjoy a more conducive environment for sharing college advice. They often work with more affluent students whose parents are college graduates. These students are going to college—it's just a matter of where.

These teenagers are also more likely to have completed rigorous college-prep classes, and their parents are more likely to have the ability to pay at least part of the college tab.

The daily grind of a counselor at a public high school, particularly in low-income areas, is starkly different from that of a counselor at a selective private high school. At many private schools, for instance, the counselor is able to devote all of his or her attention to helping students with college choices. In contrast, NACAC estimates that the typical high school counselor devotes roughly a third of his or her time to college issues.

I say all this with one caveat. You shouldn't assume that counselors at private high schools know anymore about how to pay for schools than their public school counterparts. In many cases, they are clueless. While a private counselor should be able to develop an academically tailored list of colleges for a student, he or she will probably have little or no idea whether these schools would provide the teen with merit awards or need-based financial aid.

Perhaps there is an assumption that parents whose children attend private schools can afford to pay full fare, but that is not always the case. Plenty of parents have sacrificed to send their children to private schools and consequently find it even more challenging to pay for college. Affluent families who have lived beyond their means can also be in a bind as the college years loom.

I don't think private schools are indifferent to whether their families can afford schools, but even the most conscientious counselors find it difficult to find programs that will train them in the financial aspect of college. Some universities provide college counseling certificate programs for all types of counselors—UCLA is probably the most famous—but there is not much attention devoted to financial aid. (I happen to be a graduate of UCLA's college counseling certificate program.)

Consequences of Uninformed Counselors

Ill-trained counselors, regardless of their school setting, can unintentionally create problems for families. Here are just a few examples:

Counselors typically invite local college admission reps, who have their own conflicts of interest, to be the presenters at financial aid nights. Imagine, for instance, a rep being candid and sharing with a high school audience that his university's average financial aid package is pathetic. That's never going to happen.

Counselors steer kids away from excellent schools with high price tags because they assume that families can't afford them. What they don't understand is that for some bright students, an expensive school can sometimes end up costing less than a public university.

Without understanding what the biggest sources of college money are, many counselors wrongly assume that private scholarships are the largest pot of college cash. They direct students to look for money on scholarship search engines instead of directing them to more lucrative options.

Counselors develop college lists for students without having any knowledge about whether the institutions will be generous to their teenagers.

Some counselors also encourage teenagers to apply to reach schools without appreciating the financial consequences of their advice. This can lead to teens combing *US News & World Report* to find colleges where they might barely qualify for admission. If these applicants are "lucky" enough to get into a reach school, they will usually find that the institution is unwilling to award them much, if any, money.

Action Plan

Don't assume that your high school counselors know all the answers. Consult your high school counselors, but also do your own research.

You need to investigate on your own whether the colleges on your list are financial and academic fits.

What You Need to Know About Independent College Counselors

"I believe that most of the funds expended on independent counselors are simply wasted. We do not believe they have much, if any, effect on who we accept."

—Jeffrey Brenzel, dean of undergraduate admissions at Yale University

If you want to hire the most famous private college counselors in America, it could cost you as much as a new Lexus. Or about four dozen plasma TVs. If you haven't priced this stuff lately, I'm talking about hiring college consultants in the $40,000 price range and up.

BusinessWeek once interviewed teenagers whose parents sprung for these platinum-priced counselors. They didn't want their names divulged. Perhaps they were embarrassed that their parents were spending the equivalent of a year's tuition at Harvard to, well, to get them into Harvard. The parents, however, weren't shy about writing the checks.

These hired guns don't seem to lack for clients. To accommodate the demand, one highly sought-after counselor takes the overflow from her practice and funnels them into expensive application boot camps.

The parents willing and able to write these monster checks are clearly aiming for schools that deliver the wow factor. Wealthy parents are willing to spend the big bucks to get their kids into Harvard, Princeton, Penn, or one of the other super elite schools that are magnets for the children of oil sheiks, hedge fund managers, and Hollywood stars.

It's amusing that the people who seem the most agitated about these consultants are the very people guarding the palace doors of the Ivies and the tiny fraction of other schools that reject nearly all their applicants. The chapter began with a quote from the admission dean at Yale, and I assume he would agree with what Thomas H. Parker, dean of admission and financial aid at Amherst College, had to say when he protested the use of college consultants in a piece in *The Chronicle of Higher Education*:

> *What is important to understand about families who make use of independent college counselors is that they are both highly competitive and used to controlling their own destinies. In their eyes, the college-admissions process is reduced to little more than a contest. Furthermore, it is a contest that is to be won (perhaps at all costs) and a process that is to be tightly controlled.*

Read that passage again and ask yourself if the Amherst dean couldn't be describing the motivation and behavior of his own elite college admission peers.

Protests from Elite Schools

I find it ironic that administrators at the most prestigious schools are protesting so vigorously since they are responsible for most of the nation's admission hysteria. Children who are anointed each year by the admission staff at the Harvards of the world, do need to be nearly perfect—at least using the cramped definition of perfection that elite schools use. And the odds of being anointed by these admission gods keep declining as some of these elite schools insist on encouraging ever more students to apply so they can generate even greater rejection rates.

The only people who can really play this admission game at the highest level are the wealthy. So, of course, they are going to hire people to help them with the college process just as they employ people to walk their Shih-Tzus, massage their backs, and carry their golf clubs. It's the use of these exorbitantly compensated hired guns that creates the impression that only the wealthy can win this race. And that's probably what motivates the elite schools to protest. Nobody wants to be considered a playground for the rich even when it's true.

It's easy to wag a finger at the highest-priced counselors, but frankly they are just charging what the market will bear. I also don't find it disturbing that rich people are aiming for what they want (it's the behavior of the elite schools that bothers me), but I do think it's unfortunate that the vast majority of independent college consultants get characterized as hired guns for the rich.

Very few college consultants charge anywhere approaching the high fees that capture the attention of the media. Most consultants don't consider it their job to get children into the schools that enjoy a lock on the highest college rankings.

I'd argue that most college consultants are motivated to find the best academic fit for their clients regardless of whether their clients are academic superstars or barely maintaining a 3.0 GPA. And that, by the way, is not an easy task. These consultants have to work with teenagers who don't know what they want, and why should they since they are only 17 and 18 years old. They also have to work with parents whose objectives could be clashing with their children's.

These consultants can also encounter problems dealing with high school counselors, who tend to distrust private consultants. In fact, school counselors can be resentful that families have sought outside help.

Ego might play some part in this friction. It's only natural for high school counselors to wonder why families are looking elsewhere for help. Aren't they good enough? But as you learned in the previous chapter, high school counselors are not only overwhelmed, but often don't have the knowledge to help their charges make intelligent college decisions. And frankly, some independent counselors don't either.

At least college consultants aren't distracted with having to deal with discipline problems, school bureaucracy, class scheduling, and other administrative work that high school counselors must handle. Consultants can focus on getting their clients into appropriate colleges.

Why Use an Independent College Counselor?

Independent counselors can be a valuable resource for families as they tackle a confusing process. Not all families wish to navigate the Byzantine world of college admissions by themselves.

While elite schools argue that families can manage the process by themselves, they ignore this fact: Colleges operate as businesses, and their No. 1 priority is always going to be their own institutions. So why shouldn't families who have the resources hire someone who can make the playing field a little less one sided?

The Ideal Independent College Counselor

When searching for an independent college counselor, don't be mesmerized by a firm's touted success rate in getting kids into the Ivy League. High-profile counselors aren't turning "B" students into kids that Princeton will drool over. These advisors help academic overachievers who could get into excellent schools without anyone's help. The aim of these admissions power brokers is arguably to take top students and turn them into the collegiate version of Stepford Wives to boost their chances even more. Under the circumstance, the success rate is meaningless.

The ideal counselors—and plenty are out there—spend time learning about their clients and then exploring what kind of institutions would be best for them academically, socially, geographically, and financially.

Counselors, who peddle prestige and try to Botox every blemish off a kid's record rather than finding the best fit, encourage what amounts to "child abuse." That's the opinion of Carolyn Z. Lawrence, an independent college counselor whom I respect in San Diego County. If a counselor promises she can mold a kid into the perfect candidate, Lawrence says, you should run.

Producing the perfect teenager all too often requires children to surrender much of their high school lives. These kids are pressured to take as many Advanced Placement classes as possible and maintain a grueling extracurricular schedule that consumes far too much time and provokes too much anxiety.

What Independent College Counselors Can Do

Here are some of the things that independent college counselors can help families with:

- Explain the different types of schools available.
- Develop a list of potential colleges and universities.
- Provide college-essay advice.
- Keep a student on track with applications, college research, and essays.
- Give advice on extracurriculars, internships, and summer programs.
- Review college applications.
- Provide SAT/ACT strategies.

What's also important, as far as I'm concerned, is finding a consultant who understands the financial end of paying for college. I'd highly recommend selecting someone who can help you evaluate whether schools will give your teenager need-based financial aid or merit awards. These counselors, however, are hard to find.

Unfortunately, the majority of independent college consultants are no more comfortable dealing with the financial end of college than their high school counterparts. Many consultants prefer to stick with the admission side of the equation, which is mind boggling to me. How can a consultant produce a list of potential college picks for a client without having a good idea whether the student would receive financial assistance from these schools? Ignoring the financial side of getting into college is like pitching in a baseball game with your eyes closed. It's reckless.

What is puzzling is that the organizations of private college consulting, such as the Higher Education Consultants Association and Independent Educational Consultants Association, don't require financial knowledge as a requirement for membership. The organizations seem far more focused on how many colleges a counselor has personally visited.

In their defense, these organizations argue that independent counselors will refer their clients to financial advisers who can help with the cost questions, but that's not always a satisfactory answer. First, that's one more person you have to pay, and then you have to ensure that the two experts will coordinate their efforts on your behalf. Here's the biggest potential hazard to this approach: Some so-called college financial experts are simply trying to sell parents expensive financial products such as annuities and life insurance.

Finding an Independent College Counselor

To increase your chances of finding a qualified counselor, consider looking for experts, who belong to one of these professional groups:

- American Institute of Certified Educational Planners, www.aicep.org/
- Higher Education Consultants Association, www.hecaonline.org
- Independent Educational Consultants Association, www.educationalconsulting.org
- National College Advocacy Group, www.ncagonline.org

You can search for counselors by using each of the organization's online directories.

Action Plan

Independent college counselors can be a valuable resource for families looking for assistance in the college process.

It's best to select a counselor who has a working understanding of the financial aid process.

46

Knowing What to Do When

When you come to the end of your rope, tie a knot and hang on.

—Franklin D. Roosevelt

Everybody knows that getting into college today takes work. But it's possible to reduce the stress level if you use this cheat sheet. Here's a list of what teenagers, and in some cases, their parents, should be doing beginning in the freshman year of high school.

Freshman Year

Enroll in strong college prep courses. These classes can prepare you for the workload that may await you in college. College admissions officers want to see that you've taken challenging courses. In fact, colleges routinely put more weight on grades and the strength of your high school's curriculum than they do on standardized test scores.

Meet with high school counselor. Find out what classes you need to take during the next four years to satisfy, at a minimum, the requirements of your state universities. Also ask about academic coursework that private schools might require.

Get extra help. If necessary, find a tutor for difficult subjects and/or attend summer school. Kahn Academy (www.khanacademy. org) is a great (and free) online resource for students needing help or desiring enrichment that focuses primarily on math and the sciences.

Volunteer and join. It's easy to become cynical when contemplating what extracurricular and volunteer activities are best. A teenage should not get involved in something simply because it might grab an admission officer's attention.

Colleges aren't necessarily going to be impressed if a teenager simply joins a bunch of high school clubs. They often are excited about kids who show initiative and leadership abilities. This doesn't mean that a child has to get involved in student government. Far from it. Teenagers should try linking their extracurricular activities to their passions. My daughter, for instance, had been playing soccer since third grade, so it was a natural fit for her to become a soccer coach for a kids' recreational league. She also earned money as a soccer referee for several years. In addition, she turned her love of arts and crafts into a volunteering opportunity by creating scrapbooks for assisted-living facilities.

Read, read, and read some more. Being a strong reader can not only make a teenager a better student, but it also can make it easier to perform well in college. Reading may also lead to higher scores on the SAT. Reading comprehension is not something you can cram for in the weeks leading up to the test.

Sophomore Year

Consider taking the PSAT in October. Juniors typically take this pre-SAT test, but at plenty of high schools, sophomores do as well. The test can provide an idea of how your child might fare with the SAT. By getting an assessment early, there is plenty of time to address a child's weaknesses.

Take SAT Subject Tests. If a teenager is interested in schools that require SAT Subject Tests, he or she should try to take the relevant exam right after completing the high school course. These tests are available in such courses as U.S. history, chemistry, mathematics, foreign languages, and molecular or ecological biology. Most schools don't require these extra tests, but those that do may want scores in one to three subjects.

Keep reading! Being a strong reader will help you succeed in college and, as a practical matter, should boost your chances of doing well on college standardized tests.

Start exploring schools. Books, such as *Fiske Guide to Colleges* and *The Princeton Review's The Best Colleges* Guide, provide an overview of many brand-name schools, but the vast majority of colleges and universities aren't covered. Use the website Unigo (www.unigo.com) to see what current students think of their schools. You can explore colleges at Cappex (www.cappex.com) and Zinch (www.zinch.com) that serve as handy depositories for information about schools and act as free collegiate matchmaking services. YOUniversityTV (www.youniversitytv.com) offers online tours of schools throughout the country.

Use the college search engines on the College Board website, as well as the federal College Navigator at http://nces.ed.gov/collegenavigator, to find schools. You should also visit school websites, attend college fairs in your area, and talk to your guidance counselor about potential schools.

Visit colleges. The summer between sophomore and junior year can be a convenient time to begin checking out schools. The visits may help motivate a teenager after he or she sees what hard work can lead to.

Create a filing system. Once you begin accumulating college marketing materials, you'll need a place to organize it. Create a file folder for each school that interests you.

Junior Year

Continue researching and visiting schools.

Study for the standardized tests. An inexpensive way to prepare for the test is to buy a test prep book. I particularly like the big thick books put out by the actual test makers:

> *The Real ACT Prep Guide* (CD), 3rd edition
> *The Official SAT Study Guide* with DVD

There are also plenty of free or moderately priced online test prep services and test resources. Here are some notable ones:

Grockit.com

Knewton.com

Number2.com

ePrep.com

Register for the SAT and ACT well in advance. You're taking a risk if you expect to sign up for the SAT a few days before the test. The test slots fill up, and even if you do waltz in at the last minute, the test will cost more money. You can check SAT deadlines by visiting the College Board's website.

Take the SAT. A good time for many juniors to tackle the SAT is late winter and early spring. If your child is studying Algebra II as a junior, consider delaying the test toward the end of his or her junior year since this level of math is included in the test.

Consider the ACT. Some students perform better on the ACT, while others experience greater luck on the SAT. Both test many of the same skills; however, differences exist. Unlike the SAT, for instance, the ACT includes a science section, as well as trigonometry questions. With the ACT, you need to be a fast reader. The SAT places a greater emphasis on vocabulary, and it imposes a guessing penalty.

Continue taking challenging classes.

Estimate financial aid need. Use the online Expected Family Contribution calculator that will provide your EFC (see Chapters 4, 5, and 6). Your EFC will tell you what, at a minimum, you will have to pay at any school.

Start using net price calculators. When researching schools, use a school's net price calculator, which is located on the institution's website, to get a personalized estimate of what that school will cost you. (See Chapter 7, "A Revolutionary Calculator.")

Write thank-you notes. After visiting a school, send a note if you spoke personally to an admission officer, professor, or coach.

Senior Year

Use a calendar. The more schools you apply to, the crazier it's going to get. The only way to keep track of college admissions and financial aid deadlines is by writing it all down in a calendar.

Visit schools. If you can swing it, try visiting schools before applying.

Finalize the list. Boil your list down to the serious candidates and, when applicable, decide whether to apply for early decision, early action, or regular decision.

Work on applications. In the summer months, before the senior year gets underway, write your college essays. If you are an artist, musician, or actor, you may have to send in a portfolio with your application. Summer is the time to get this finished.

Get a head start on recommendations. A lot of teachers and guidance counselors are inundated with requests for recommendations around Thanksgiving. Ask teachers for recommendations in October or even earlier when they will be less harried. Thank teachers who help with a gift certificate.

Retake the SAT and/or ACT. With deadlines looming, time is running out to take the standardized tests again if you aren't happy with your scores. Many schools will cherry pick your best SAT scores. Some institutions will do the same for the ACT.

Complete the CSS/Financial Aid PROFILE. Nearly 250 mostly private, selective schools use this online form to determine eligibility for financial aid that doesn't emanate from the state and federal governments. You can register to use the PROFILE by visiting the College Board website. The easiest way to find the application is to Google "PROFILE."

File the Free Application for Federal Student Aid (FAFSA). All schools participating in the federal financial aid program use this form. Submit the FAFSA, which is available beginning January 1 of every year.

Evaluate admissions offers. Once the admission verdicts and financial aid packages are in, families may need to do some soul searching. Parents and students should talk about the financial implications of attending different schools.

CHAPTER 46 • KNOWING WHAT TO DO WHEN   **221**

Take Advanced Placement tests. If you're doing well in Advanced Placement classes, take the appropriate AP tests that are administered in May. If you do perform well, you may obtain college credits.

Contact the also-rans. Write or email the schools that didn't make your final cut so they can extend offers to other students.

Send in deposit. For many schools, the deadline for mailing in the enrollment form with the deposit is May 1.

Don't slack off. Even after you receive college acceptances, you should keep your grades up in the last semester. Colleges can rescind offers.

Decide whether to borrow money. Use federal college loans first. Private loans should be your last option.

Register for Selective Service. Young men won't be eligible for federal financial aid if they haven't registered.

Find a summer job. Get a head start on paying those college bills.

Action Plan

Don't wait until your junior or senior year to begin preparing for college.

It will be easier to stay on top of your college to-do list if you remain organized.

47

Writing Your Way into College

Ninety percent of the applications I read contain what I call McEssays—usually five-paragraph essays that consist primarily of abstractions and unsupported generalization. They are technically correct in that they are organized and have the correct sentence structure and spelling, but they are boring.

—Parke Muth, senior assistant dean, University of Virginia

On a sunny autumn day in San Diego, scores of college guidance counselors from across the country resisted the temptation to walk along the city's gorgeous beaches. Instead they grabbed seats in a chilly, windowless room.

The counselors, who were attending the College Board's annual convention, had shown up for one reason: To learn the secrets of writing a successful college essay. Not surprisingly, the room was jammed.

With top schools so competitive, many ambitious kids assume that if they write a zinger of an essay, it might provide an admission edge. Consequently, teenagers, parents, and counselors are eager to know just what a winning essay looks like.

The speakers at the College Board session included administrators at Kenyon College in Gambier, Ohio, and Yale University in New Haven, Connecticut. The Yale presenter said the university kept 20 staffers busy reading 50 essays a day, six days a week during application season. Here is some of the advice that the speakers shared:

Avoid the thesaurus. Don't write like a pedantic humanities professor who is trying too hard to impress colleagues. Avoid ostentatious words that you would normally never touch. One presenter provided this real, over-the-top example of an overstuffed essay:

> Hi my name is Jim, and since brevity is the soul of wit I will meekly attempt to convey to you a succinct summary of my ephemeral existence. Allow me amnesty as I am often a bit alliterative. Time is of the essence throughout humankind, and with every word I write, the nearly endless ebb of extravagant expressions flow like a rushing river, fleeing futilely towards an irrelevant ocean. Dam!

Don't write like that!

Skip the English paper. Too many high school English teachers encourage their pupils to write with as much flare as a cardboard box. They don't do their students any favors by insisting that they follow stilted formulas. For instance, when students write the classic persuasive essay, they are supposed to stuff the pros and cons on a subject, whether it's abortion or a presidential election, in the very first paragraph. Students can be penalized if they deviate from that formula even if they craft a compelling essay.

High school teachers often chastise kids who dare to use "first person" in their papers. Colleges, however, are eager to experience an applicant's "voice" in an essay, which means writing in first person is essential. The Yale presenter called essays written in third person "scary."

The following opening lines from some successful application essays to Stanford University might inspire you to ditch the wooden writing:

- I have old hands.
- On a hot Hollywood evening, I sat on a bike sweltering in a winter coat and furry boots.
- I've been surfing Lake Michigan since I was three years old.
- As an Indian-American, I am forever bound to the hyphen.
- Some fathers might disapprove of their children handling noxious chemicals in the garage.
- I change my name each time I place an order at Starbucks.

- Unlike many mathematicians, I live in an irrational world; I feel that my life is defined by a certain amount of irrationalities that bloom too frequently, such as my brief foray in front of 400 people without my pants.

- When I was in eighth grade I couldn't read.

Be specific. Students tend to be vague when writing essays. A teenager might write, for instance, that his mom is "nice." Nice is a nearly meaningless adjective. When journalists interview neighbors about an apprehended serial killer, inevitably they say that he was a "nice guy." Substitute vague generalities for details, details, details.

Deliver a take-home message. You can write a serious essay, a humorous one, a clever one. There is no right way, but you have to make sure that your essay reflects back upon you. The Yale speaker observed that a lot of Ivy League wannabes write about Winston Churchill without ever tying the essay back to themselves. If you write about Darfur, what does that have to do with you? And simply writing that you feel outraged won't cut it.

Whether you are talking about cleaning a beach, babysitting, or a brush with death, the essay must provide a strong sense of self. Your personality must emerge. And it should reflect what kind of person you are now. Not the person you might have been when your house was damaged by a hurricane when you were ten-years-old or when you got lost at Disneyland at the age of six.

At the College Board session, the experts shared examples of amusing essays that were entertaining—and would have worked—if each of them had conveyed what kind of person the writer was. One essay involved a guy whose last name was Weiner. As in hot dog. The essay was quite clever, but it was missing that one key element.

Stay away from the pack. I once heard an administrator at the University of San Diego speak about the thousands of college essays that he'd read over the years. What irritated him was the tendency of high schoolers to embrace the same hackneyed subjects.

Each year, applicants deluge USD's admission office with essays about volunteering to build houses for poor families in Tijuana. Obviously, this is a regional phenomenon with students from Southern

California, but in every region of the country, teenagers are writing essays about subjects that have been covered ad nauseam.

Here's the administrator's other pet peeve: Teens writing about their sports teams. And he is hardly alone. Frankly, nobody is going to care—except a college's athletic coaches—if you kicked the winning soccer goal at an important tournament or you swatted more home runs than anybody in your high school's history.

Once again, what matters is composing an essay that speaks to who you are.

Don't be careless. More than 450 schools, almost all private, allow students to apply to colleges by filling out just one standardized form via the Common Application (www.commonapp.org). Obviously, completing one application for multiple schools cuts down on the hassle factor. Even better, a student can use one essay to satisfy the writing requirement for all these schools.

The one-stop application process, however, can cause students to make embarrassing mistakes. Admission officers everywhere can tell you about teenagers who express their deep desire to attend a competing school in their essay. These applicants forgot to swap out the name of one school for another before sending the application electronically.

Action Plan

Don't assume that your essay should be written like an English paper. Write from your heart and rely on details when you tell your story.

48

Visiting College Campuses

Welcome, prospective students. I'm here to show you a very superficial version of what your life could be like for the next four years because I need the money.

—Anonymous tour guide, CollegeHumor.com

Is there a strategy to deciding which colleges to visit?

I received that question once from a California mom who visited my blog, The College Solution. She was particularly interested in whether her daughter should visit state universities in California, even though her daughter wouldn't get any brownie points from the schools for touring their campuses. She was wondering if the time would be better spent traveling to distant private colleges where the family's visits would be appreciated and possibly even rewarded with a greater chance of admission or even merit money.

The mom also wanted to know what I had done with my own children and whether we had visited schools before applying.

My son and daughter applied only to colleges that they had first visited. By checking out schools in advance, they were able to eliminate those that didn't appear to be good all-around fits. Visits are also a good way to help judge whether a school is worth its price tag. Some of this winnowing, by the way, seemed awfully subjective to my husband and me, but we kept our mouths shut.

We didn't have the time or money to visit schools in every region that my children had an interest. There are obviously many families who face the same constraint. My daughter, for instance, never got a chance to look at Midwestern schools. She visited colleges in the

Pacific Northwest on a summer trip and she headed to the East Coast the following year. My son visited fewer schools, but he was able to check out schools in the Pacific Northwest, as well as the East and West coasts.

If we had waited until our teenagers had received acceptance letters to visit schools, we wouldn't have had much time. Acceptances often arrive in March and April, and the deposit deadline is typically May 1.

So what did I tell the mom who asked if there was any strategy involved in visiting schools? I suggested that it made more sense for the family to visit the distant private schools first. These schools are more likely to reward students who have shown a "demonstrated interest" in their institutions (see Chapter 19, "Showing a College Some Love"). In contrast, it would be easier to squeeze in visits to state schools before an admission decision needs to be made.

Eight Things to Know Before Visiting a College

Here are eight pieces of advice to consider when contemplating college trips:

1. **Think about timing.** Sure, visiting schools during the summer is convenient for students, but don't expect to encounter the real college experience. Many colleges, for example, will be just about deserted. And don't assume that universities will exude the same feel that you'd get on an autumn day or the first warm day in spring when the quadrangle is packed with sunbathers.

   If you plan a visit when a school is in session, you may be able to arrange for your child to spend the night in a dorm and sit in on classes. Colleges and universities generally recommend that you contact them two weeks in advance to book tour reservations. The easiest way to learn about a college's visitation opportunities is to check its website.

2. **Take notes.** If you visit more than a couple of campuses during a trip, the details will blur quickly. Which school, you may wonder, said 95% of its students receive some sort of financial aid or academic grants? Which one boasted that 60% of its students study abroad? If your child doesn't take notes, she might end up only remembering things that don't mean squat. My daughter, for example, remembered that the turkey sandwich she inhaled at the cafeteria at Willamette University in Salem, Oregon, tasted better than the one she ate at Whitman College in Walla Walla, Washington.

   Urge your child to write down his or her observations after each visit. A good time to do that is in the car while driving to the next college.

3. **Don't overdo it.** Logistically, it's going to be impossible to visit more than two campuses in one day. And you'll only be able to squeeze in one campus a day if your child intends to take a tour, show up for an information session, meet with an admission officer, and attend a class.

4. **Know your place.** Parents, who are often the ones bankrolling a child's education, may be eager to ask questions during campus tours. But it's best to encourage your child to be the one posing most of them.

5. **Write a note.** When my children returned from college tours, they wrote thank-you notes to the admission officers that they met.

6. **Lighting a fire.** Ultimately, a college trip should help your child become acquainted with what lies ahead. It may motivate him or her to focus on the ultimate prize—finding a great academic fit at a reasonable price.

7. **Ways to cut travel costs.** To shrink costs on trips, I always bid for hotels and cars on Priceline. I never accept a hotel's published price on Priceline, but instead I offer a low-ball price through the site's bidding process. Sometimes I get a cheap price right away, and other times I have to keep offering low bids for a few days.

8. **Try virtual tours.** Don't feel badly if you can't afford to visit as many schools as you'd like. A student can compensate by making sure a school knows he's interested. Schools often track every contact a child or parent makes with the institution, whether it's a request for literature, a call to the admission office, or a conversation during a college fair.

You can get an idea of what schools look like by taking virtual tours, which many colleges offer on their websites. Another source of college videos is YOUniversityTV.com. Also take advantage of a school's Facebook and other social media sites. You can also request to talk with current students at the school.

Action Plan

To get the most out of your visits, plan well enough ahead and don't rush through the time spent on campuses.

Think strategically when selecting which schools to visit.

49

Acing the College Interview

A student who doesn't take the time to visit the campus and schedule an interview is sending us a message that they are not very interested in us.

—An admission director at Gettysburg College

During an interview at Dickinson College in Pennsylvania, Seth Allen, who was the school's head of admissions and is now the admissions dean at Pomona College, asked my daughter, Caitlin, this question: "What is the most creative thought that you've ever had?"

Caitlin's first panicked thought was this: "What? I have no idea."

Then her brain kicked in and she blurted out something about chopsticks. She told Allen that she wanted to learn how to use chopsticks with her left hand because she thought this would impress colleges.

Was this a silly answer? Absolutely. But Caitlin figured that answering the question was far better than hemming and hawing and ultimately punting on it. And looking back, she believes that this was the turning point in the interview. Allen seemed to be intrigued by my gregarious daughter's enthusiasm for eating Kung Pao chicken left-handed, and he continued to ask her questions 35 minutes longer than the interview was scheduled to last.

I share this anecdote to drive home this point: There aren't necessarily right and wrong answers in a college interview. Admission officers don't want kids to fail. They like teenagers or they would have chosen another occupation.

What admission staffers strive to extract from kids is a sense of who they are. They want their personality to shine through. Did my daughter even intend to practice eating left-handed? No. But what her answer and the others she provided during the interview showed was that she is self-confident, a quick thinker, and an entertaining story-teller. It wasn't so much what she said, but how she said it. Months later, she received an acceptance letter from Dickinson, along with a scholarship.

What You Need to Know About Interviews

As you anticipate spending face time with admission officers or alumni representatives, here are some things to keep in mind to increase your chances of having productive and successful interviews:

Ask about interview opportunities. College interviews aren't as commonplace as they used to be when the parents of today's teen-agers were applying to college. There are far more students heading to college now, and the crush of applications makes interviews infea-sible at many schools.

Interviews, however, remain popular at colleges that are able to take a holistic approach to their admissions process. It's a way that a college can get a sense about whether a student would be a good fit for their institution. The staff can take the time to sit down and chat with teenagers because they process far fewer applications than a university.

While staffers at colleges often conduct their own interviews with prospective students, alumni often are responsible for interviews for students applying to private universities. How important these inter-views are varies by school, but if a university recommends one, you should make every effort to schedule an interview.

Public universities don't have the luxury of conducting one-on-one interviews with potential students. Because of the large numbers of applicants, their admission policies are often largely dictated by the numbers—a child's grade point average, standardized test scores, and class rank.

Don't assume you have to visit the school. College interviews aren't always held on campuses. College reps, particularly in the fall, fan out to different regions to conduct interviews, as well as visit high schools and other venues. Sometimes these reps conduct interviews in hotel conference rooms. Universities often use alumni to conduct interviews throughout the country.

Some colleges and universities even maintain full-time reps stationed in other regions. Dozens of admission reps from state and private colleges and universities outside California, for instance, belong to the Regional Admission Counselors of California. Schools that participate in RACC include Arizona State University, University of Arizona, Brandeis University, Franklin & Marshall College, Oregon State University, Seton Hall University, University of Michigan, University of Minnesota, Whitman College, and William Woods University.

An easy way to find out about interview opportunities is to head to a school's admission home page. On the site, you will often see a calendar of events, near and far, that admission reps will be attending. If, for instance, you live in Seattle and you discover that a liberal arts college in Ohio will be visiting your city, email the school's admission rep for the state of Washington and ask about connecting. You will get brownie points for contacting the rep, who more than likely will be the counselor who first reviews your application. Getting to know this person is to your benefit.

Pinpoint the type of interview. Prepare for the right kind of interview. Some schools use informational interviews that allow students to ask admission staffers about their institutions. Typically, the admission officer does not fill out a written evaluation of the meeting so your admission file will not mention what took place.

In contrast, many schools rely on an evaluative interview. These interviews can be stressful because the admission officer will typically write an interview summary afterward. At these schools, the interview is just one of many factors that are considered for admission.

Ask intelligent questions. The best way to sabotage an interview is to show up knowing little about the school. If your knowledge of a school is nil, an admission officer is going to wonder why you're wasting his time. What's more, interviews aren't one sided. While you will be expected to answer questions, this is also a time for you to elicit information about the campus from your host. If you don't know enough to ask intelligent questions, you're in trouble. Arrive to the interview with at least three solid questions to ask.

While you might want to know whether the school has a vegan meal plan or which is the best dorm, often the most valuable questions go unasked. A source for more insightful questions comes from the National Survey of Student Engagement, based at Indiana University in Bloomington, that explores what educational activities are most effective.

NSSE's brochure *A Pocket Guide to Choosing a College: Are You Asking the Right Questions?* contains questions about student and faculty interactions, academic workload, class collaboration, and more. You can download the brochure after Googling the title.

Dress appropriately. There's definitely no need to wear a suit or tie at interviews, but you should look like a well-dressed teenager wearing comfortable clothes. I heard this great recommendation once: Dress as if you were going out to lunch with your grandparents.

Watch the slang. Don't pepper your conversation with "um," "you know," and "like." Practice ahead of time to try to eliminate these sorts of words from your conversation. And during interviews, don't slouch, stare at the floor, play with your hair, or display other nervous mannerisms.

Be yourself. Don't pretend to love Leo Tolstoy and William Shakespeare if you're into science fiction novels and Japanese comic books. Resist trying to figure out what you suspect are the "right" answers; you don't want to sound phony. The interview is a time to brag about what you've accomplished without sounding conceited. On the flip side, you should put the best light on any black marks tarnishing your record, such as a "D" in an honors calculus class. And before the interview starts, take a deep breath!

Book an interview. A college admission officer can tell you whether an interview is important. If it is, you should make every attempt to arrange an interview either at the campus, on Skype, or through regional reps or alumni in your area. It's really inexcusable to not visit a campus and sit through an interview if you live within several hours of a school. The admission staff will wonder why you didn't make the effort, and it could hurt your chances.

Action Plan

Find out whether the schools that you are interested in require or recommend interviews. If they do, make sure to arrange one.

Research a school before an interview and be prepared to ask intelligent questions.

50

Transferring to a Different College

Without some assistance, transfer students are like Alice in Wonderland. They go from one place to another and have no clue about the culture of the institution.

—Alfred Herrera, assistant vice provost, UCLA

A college freshman who hoped to transfer to an Ivy League school turned one day to College Confidential, a popular online college forum, to ask for advice.

The student shared with the group that she had slacked off during her junior year in high school and therefore her grades (3.6 GPA) weren't good enough to get into an Ivy League school. She had only been attending a college in Texas for a couple of months, but she was eager to transfer to any Ivy League school after she earned excellent grades in her midterm exams.

Members of the forum gave her lots of advice and encouragement on how to transfer into Ivy League schools. I found it all quite strange. Transferring into an Ivy League university is tough and in some cases even more difficult than applying as a high school senior. Harvard's transfer admittance rate, for instance, is 1%.

No one urged the girl to make the most of her current college, much less suggest the futility of what she was aiming to do. Nor did anyone question her motivation for desiring to attend one of these institutions. Her rationale for wanting to move east: "I always wanted to go to an Ivy League school."

Pretty compelling reason, huh?

Not all students who hope to transfer from one four-year school to another are pursuing a quixotic dream. Many students possess solid reasons, including financial ones, to transfer. And, of course, the aim of community college students who desire a bachelor's degree is to eventually transfer to a four-year school.

While you rarely hear much about transfer students, about one out of three students who are enrolled in either a four-year or two-year institution will end up transferring.

Many years ago, I was one of those transfer students. I started out as a history major at the University of Missouri in St. Louis, which was just one and a half blocks from our home. It was the most economical option for my parents, who put all five of their children through college. After discovering at the commuter school that my real passion was journalism, I transferred as a junior to the University of Missouri in Columbia, which is the home of the nation's oldest journalism school. My experience at both schools worked out beautifully for me.

Transferring Chances

If you are interested in transferring, the good news is that nearly all schools welcome transfer students. The transfer acceptance rate, according to a report from the National Association for College Admission Counseling, is not much lower than the rate for freshmen.

Actually, a growing number of colleges and universities actively recruit transfer students. In some cases, schools are looking to replenish their student bodies as hard economic times have caused some students to drop out. Interest in transfer students has also grown as the number of college-age students in this country has dropped. Iowa State University, for instance, built a transfer program to capture more students in a state with a declining number of teenagers.

What You Need to Know

If you plan to transfer from a community college or a four-year institution, you need to be prepared. Here are some of the things you should know:

Determine your odds. When drawing up a list of possible transfer schools, you should appreciate in advance what kind of odds you face. Universities, which are by nature larger, are more equipped to accept greater numbers of transfer students. The University of California, Berkeley, for example, recently accepted 3,451 transfer students, which represents a 23% transfer acceptance rate. The University of Texas, Austin, accepted 41% of its transfer applicants. while Georgetown University, which has a robust transfer program in place, accepted 22.5%, which was just a couple of percentage points lower than its freshman admittance rate.

Among the schools that are the toughest to crack are small elite colleges where there is little student attrition. For instance, the transfer acceptance rate at Amherst College was recently less than 6%. The freshman acceptance rate at this elite school was 15%. The odds get significantly better as the selectivity of a school declines. About a half-hour drive from Amherst, Western New England University, for example, accepted 63% of its transfer applicants.

How can you tell whether a school welcomes a significant number of transfer applicants? It's easy. Head to the College Board's BigFuture website (http://bigfuture.org). Once on the site, you can call up the profile of any school by typing its name in the search box. On the left-hand side of a school's profile, you'll see the For Transfer Students link. Click on the link and you'll find the number of transfer students who applied, were admitted, and enrolled. Just as importantly, you will discover what the admission requirements are for transfer students. These are the sorts of admission requirements that you will find:

- Essay
- Recommendations
- Transcript
- Statement of good standing from current school
- Maximum allowable transferable credits from current institution
- Minimum college grade point average
- Lowest grade allowed for any transferable course credits

The College Board profile also shares what level of student is eligible to transfer. At some schools, for instance, second semester freshmen are eligible to transfer while other schools consider only sophomores or juniors.

As a general rule, the longer you have attended college, the less important your high school grade point average and SAT/ACT scores will be to a new school. This is good news for students who would prefer to bury their high school records.

Be prepared for colleges and universities to ask why you want to transfer. Focus on the positive reasons why you desire change. You should not complain about your current school.

Is the school transfer friendly? Unfortunately, some institutions take the position that transfer students don't need any special accommodations because they aren't college newbies. That's a misguided attitude, but it's all too common.

One indication that a school will be transfer friendly is if it has a transfer coordinator. Another good sign: the school provides a transfer orientation or other programs specifically designed for transfer students There is a growing trend for universities to offer special transition courses. UCLA, for example, provides a class for transfer students called Life Skills for College Students.

Some large schools have created transfer centers to create a home for new students as they acclimate to their campuses. The University of Arizona, for instance, created a transfer center within its student union building. It also shows an institutional commitment when a university offers transfer housing to students.

Before making your decision, you ideally should talk to transfer students to hear about their experiences at specific schools.

What will this school cost? Before getting excited about the prospects of transferring, check what a move would cost. An excellent way to do this is to use a school's net price calculator for transfer students. By federal law, every school must have a net price calculator installed on its website for freshmen and transfer students. (See Chapter 7, "A Revolutionary Calculator".) A calculator will provide a student with a personalized estimate of what a particular school will cost. I would not advise applying to any schools unless you have run the numbers.

Transfer students typically don't receive as much need-based financial aid as first-year students. Schools like to reserve their best packages for high school seniors where the competition for new students is keenest. That said, financial aid certainly is available for transfer students, but the amounts vary significantly.

In addition to institutional money, private scholarships exist specifically for transfer students. For instance, Phi Theta Kappa, an academic honor society for two-year college students, is a notable source for private scholarships. It awards more than $1 million in scholarships annually and partners with more than 700 institutions that dispense in excess of $37 million to the honor society's members. The Jack Kent Cooke Foundation is another top source of transfer scholarships.

Making the Most of Your New School

Once you are settled in at your new school, make the most of it. Studies show that transfer students are less likely to take advantage of the many opportunities that their new schools offer. They are less likely to participate in such high-impact activities as studying abroad, internships, senior projects, and undergraduate research. Don't let that be you.

Action Plan

Research which schools are transfer friendly and make sure that you understand the cost before making the move.

51

Getting Credit for Your Work

Many four-year institutions do not inform their admitted transfer students how their credits will transfer until these students are well into their first term at the senior institution.

—College Board's Improving Student Transfer from Community Colleges to Four-Year Institutions

A few years ago, the daughter of a friend of mine decided pretty much on a whim that she wanted to transfer to New York University.

She was a first-semester junior at the University of San Francisco when she decided to apply to NYU. She was accepted, and during the holidays, she moved to Manhattan and, voilà, was an NYU undergrad.

She was excited about the move until she discovered that NYU wasn't going to accept a significant number of her credits. After one semester in Manhattan, she transferred back to USF.

For those who want to transfer to another college or university, the process is trickier than applying for a freshman class. A chief reason is because the transfer requirements vary from school to school. Even within a university, the transfer requirements can differ within departments.

In contrast, high school students know that if they take college prep classes, perform well in school, and earn decent standardized test scores, many schools would be happy to accept them into their freshman class.

In an interview conducted for a College Board report, a UCLA administrator summed up the challenge transfer students face at just the nine campuses within the University of California system:

One of the main differences between freshmen and transfer applicants is a freshman knows he or she has to do four years of English composition and all of the other college-prep courses to go to any of our campuses. A transfer applicant, however, must focus on prerequisite courses that will prepare him or her for a particular major. But the reality is we have nine different undergraduate campuses and there could be nine different kinds of patterns of preparation for any given major.

Preserving Credits

The trickiest part of transferring to another school is preserving your academic credits. Unfortunately, students often are so eager to move to a new school that they don't think about losing credits that they worked so diligently to earn.

Ideally, attaining an associate's degree should fulfill the requirements for the first two years of a baccalaureate degree. In many states, however, graduates can't assume that a four-year institution will honor all their credits. Four-year institutions maintain their own requirements for which community college credits transfer.

So how do you know whether your dream school will take your credits? Students starting out at community colleges can pick a school that maintains well-established relations with the college or university that they hope to eventually attend. For instance, the University of California system, which has a highly competitive admissions policy for freshmen, offers a popular program for the state's community college students. The vast majority of students who transfer to the UC campuses come from the state's community colleges.

The relationship between community campuses and four-year institutions is spelled out in so-called articulation agreements. In some states, such as Florida and Pennsylvania, anybody who graduates with an associate's degree in these states will be welcomed into a four-year public school in their respective state.

You can obtain a state-by-state list of articulation agreements by visiting the website of FinAid (www.finaid.org). Type "articulation agreement" into FinAid's search box to locate the list.

Some articulation agreements also include private four-year schools. You can find partnerships between community colleges and private colleges and universities across the country. The University of Southern California and Mount St. Mary's College, which are both in Los Angeles, for instance, honor agreements with many community colleges in California. In Pennsylvania, community colleges maintain articulation agreements with dozens of private institutions in the Keystone State such as Bucknell University, Duquesne University, Widener University, Lehigh University, Lafayette College, University of Scranton, and Villanova University.

Transferring from a Four-Year Institution

If you want to hop from one four-year school to another, making sure credits transfer is obviously just as important. You should talk to a transfer credit evaluator at the school you hope to attend to determine what credits you can preserve. You should do the same if you are heading from a two-year to a four-year school.

Making sure a four-year institution will accept your credits shouldn't be your only goal. You also want to ask the transfer credit evaluator how you can determine whether the credits will apply to your intended major.

Action Plan

It's critically important for students to find out whether their credits will be honored when they transfer to another college or university.

Part VI

Borrowing for College

52

The Best Student Loans

The growth in education debt is like cooking a lobster. The increase in total student debt occurs slowly but steadily; by the time you notice that the water is boiling, you're already cooked.

—Mark Kantrowitz, publisher of FinAid.org

Americans owe more on their student loans than they do on credit card debt. Mind boggling, isn't it?

Students have been borrowing an increasing amount of money to finance their education. Student debt, which has exceeded credit card debt, is nearing the trillion-dollar mark.

About two-thirds of students borrow for college, and graduates are leaving school with more than $25,000 in debt. This figure, by the way, doesn't include the money that parents borrow to help their children.

Is $25,000 a reasonable amount of debt? It depends upon what type of student loan an undergrad selects. I agree with Lauren Asher, president of The Project on Student Debt, who once observed, "How you borrow, not just how much you borrow, really matters."

If you must borrow, you need to understand which loans are worth pursuing. Luckily, it isn't difficult to locate the best loans to pay for a degree.

The Smart Way to Borrow for College

Here's what you need to know about borrowing intelligently.

Use federal student loans first. Federal student loans are the superior choice for families, and, by far, the Direct Stafford Loan is the best one. Here are the top benefits of a Stafford Loan:

- Fixed interest rate.
- Borrowers receive same rate regardless of credit score.
- Repayment plan allows qualified borrowers to pay back loans based on their current income, not the amount they owe.
- Eligible borrowers can participate in a public service student loan forgiveness program.

In contrast to private loans, federal loans provide lower interest rates and fixed monthly payments. What's more, federal loans offer repayment programs based on a graduate's income. This program is called Income-Based Repayment, and if your federal student loan debt exceeds your annual income, you may benefit from the program. Stafford borrowers can also obtain deferments for financial hardships, and cancellation provisions exist if the borrower dies or becomes totally and permanently disabled.

There are two types of Stafford Loans—subsidized and unsubsidized. The subsidized Stafford, which is reserved for needier students, is more attractive because the government pays the interest while the student remains in school. In contrast, the interest on the unsubsidized Stafford begins accruing after the loan documents are signed. If the borrower does not pay the interest as it accrues, the interest is capitalized, adding it to the loan balance.

The interest rate on unsubsidized Stafford Loans is currently 6.8% with a one-time 1% fee based on the loan amount. The subsidized Stafford Loan has traditionally offered a lower interest rate, though at the time this book was being published, the rate was scheduled to rise to the same level as the unsubsidized version.

There is a limit to how much you can borrow through Stafford Loans. Here are the ceilings for dependent students:

Freshman: $5,500

Sophomore: $6,500

Junior: $7,500

Senior: $7,500

Dependent students can borrow a maximum of $31,000 through Stafford Loans, and no more than $23,000 can be in subsidized loans. Independent students can borrow up to $57,500, with no more than $23,000 being subsidized.

To qualify for the Stafford or any other federal college loans, a family must complete the Free Application for Federal Student Aid (FAFSA). Based on the FAFSA results, schools notify a student if they qualify for a subsidized Stafford Loan.

Generally you have 10 to 30 years to repay these loans, and the payments need to start six months after you graduate, leave school, or drop below half-time enrollment.

Direct PLUS Loan for Parents

Many families won't be able to borrow all that they need through a Stafford, but they can through the federal Direct PLUS Loan for Parents. While the Stafford is reserved for students, the PLUS Loan is designed for moms and dads. Parents can borrow enough to meet the cost of a school's attendance that isn't covered by their child's financial aid package. Unlike a Stafford, there is no set borrowing limit.

The interest rate for the federal PLUS Loan is 7.9%, and there is an additional 4% fee based on the loan amount. Parents may start repaying the PLUS debt 60 days after the loan is dispersed, or they can defer the payments until six months after the child's graduation.

Parents will qualify for a PLUS Loan unless they have an adverse credit history that includes filing for bankruptcy, having a foreclosure or repossession in the last five years, or having bills that are at least 90 days overdue.

Parents who own homes should compare the fixed rate of a PLUS, along with its fees, with another alternative—a home equity line of credit. They also need to plug potential tax breaks into this equation. Parents can deduct home equity interest off their taxes if they itemize, but they may also qualify for an above-the-line tax deduction for college loan interest even if they don't itemize.

For parents who don't own a home or who have little home equity, the PLUS Loan is a no-brainer compared to signing a private loan, which should be your last resort.

Be Realistic About What You Borrow

This may sound cruel, but if you aspire to be a paralegal or a painter, you probably shouldn't be borrowing as much as a future dermatologist or investment banker. Here's a handy rule of thumb: Don't borrow more than your anticipated starting salary after you graduate. If you borrow more than twice your starting salary, it's likely that you will be in extreme financial difficulty and will struggle to make the monthly payments.

Action Plan

The federal Stafford Loan is preferable to other college loans. For many parents, the PLUS Loan will be the next best loan to tap for college.

53

Private College Loan Perils

*A family taking out a $12,000 private loan is paying $5,000
more in interest because the parents aren't taking 30 minutes
to shop and they only complete one application.*

—Sue Kim, CEO of Alltuition.com

The director of financial aid at Barnard College became concerned years ago when she was examining figures on the number of students at the women's college who were obtaining private loans.

Administrators in Barnard's financial aid office understood why private loans should be a last resort. But the school's parents didn't appreciate the potential hazards of a private loan.

Consequently, the school in New York City instituted a policy that requires contacting families who are on the verge of assuming a private loan. After conversations with Barnard staffers, families often abandon their plan to rely on a private loan. During the first year it was implemented, private-loan volume at the school dropped from $1.6 million to $400,000.

The Hazards of Private College Loans

Private loans, as the Barnard families learned, should be the last resort. Here are some reasons why:

Private loans charge variable interest rates. Private loan payments, which may initially seem manageable, are subject to change because most private loans include variable interest rates that lack a ceiling cap. You may be paying off a private loan for ten years or more, and no one knows what will happen to interest rates.

Not everybody receives the same deal. Borrowers participating in the federal loan program all receive the same rates, but this isn't true with private loans. Families with excellent credit can obtain lower interest rates than those whose credit rating is not as good. The spread between the starting interest rates for stellar customers versus those stuck with the worst rates can be 10 percentage points or more.

In addition, the interest rates and fees of private loans can vary from school to school. Some lenders take into account an institution's overall loan default rate. So even if you have an unblemished credit history, you could still get penalized.

Private loans can be confusing. I suspect that many people who end up with a private loan don't even know what kind they have. Sometimes families don't realize what they've got until later when they try to consolidate the debt with federal loans. You can't combine private and federal loans when consolidating, which is another knock against the private variety. How is this confusion possible? Families, after surviving the college admission process, may hardly be in the mood to sort through loan possibilities in the spring and summer leading up to a child's freshman year. Parents and students just want the cash and figure they'll worry about how to pay it back later. Obviously not a good idea.

When Considering a Private Student Loan

If you're considering a private loan, here is what you should be doing:

Use federal loans first. Families should not turn to private loans, also called alternative loans, unless they have maxed out the federal Direct Stafford Loan (see the previous chapter), which offers better terms and preferable repayment options. Many families inadvertently fail to exhaust their Stafford option before turning to private loans.

As I also mentioned in the previous chapter, parents should seriously consider borrowing through the federal Direct PLUS Loan for Parents. The PLUS Loan doesn't have the desirable repayment options that the Stafford offers, but the interest rate is fixed.

Check with credit unions. Credit unions, which are newer players in the private student loan arena, almost always provide better interest rates. You can learn more about credit union student loans and apply by visiting cuStudentLoans.org. Ironically, many people gravitate to the big name lenders even though they are less likely to offer attractive rates. Also check with state loan programs, which sometimes offer much better rates than commercial lenders.

Be skeptical of the advertised rate. Lenders attempt to attract customers by advertising their lowest rate that's actually reserved for parents with impeccable credit histories. Don't be fooled. Mark Kantrowitz, the publisher of FinAid.org, estimates that less than 5% of borrowers capture the best rate. At the time I was finishing this book, for instance, Sallie Mae, a major lender, was advertising its best rate at 3%, but the average borrowers were paying 9% to 10% interest, according to AllTuition.com, which operates a private student-loan comparison site.

Apply for multiple loans. When I talked with Sue Kim, the chief executive officer of AllTuition.com, she told me that comparison shoppers on her site check out many loans but then rarely apply for more than one. Unfortunately, there is a lack of transparency in up-front pricing, which means that there is no way to tell which loans will provide the best rates without applying. When you apply for multiple loans, you can choose the one that comes back with the best terms. Over the life of a loan, you could save yourself many thousands of dollars.

Don't get tricked by slick marketers. Lenders' marketing materials make it seem as if obtaining a private loan is as easy as ordering Chinese takeout. Here's an excerpt from a letter sent by Sallie Mae that I received a couple of months before my daughter began college: "Classes will start again before you know it. Don't let worrying about college expenses ruin your summer.... Applying is fast, free, and easy. Borrow up to $40,000 a year."

Sallie Mae went on to promise that my husband and I wouldn't have to worry about filling out any federal financial aid forms! Many parents might think that is a plus, but the lender was recklessly providing families with a way to jeopardize their chances for the best financial aid. Parents should fill out the federal form—FAFSA—because without doing so, they can't obtain federal loans, which are far preferable.

All the junk mail I received from lenders made private loans seem like the best, easiest approach by offering, in the words of one lender, "fast" credit decisions, "quick" renewals, and "easy" online applications. The promises sound great, but the price you pay will be high.

Make timely payments. You never want to court trouble with any college lender. One of the best ways to avoid punitive penalties for missing payments is to sign up for automatic payments through your checking or savings account. Many people mess up when they change residences, and they fail to receive their bill.

Don't overborrow. Parents who are borrowing for college should not forget about their own retirement. Don't overcommit financially. Parents should not borrow more than they can afford to repay in ten years.

Action Plan

Never choose a private loan unless you have maxed out your federal loans.

If you want to appreciate what can happen if you borrow too much for college, head to StudentLoanJustice.org, which contains countless horror stories of student borrowers.

Index

University of Nevada, 43
University of New Mexico, 43
University of North Carolina, 34, 51, 108, 132, 135, 191
University of North Dakota, 35, 41
University of Notre Dame, 4-5, 12, 117, 175, 191
University of Oklahoma, 35-36
University of Oregon, 34-35, 38, 42, 172
University of Pennsylvania, 12, 121, 175, 176, 181, 191
University of Puerto Rico, 118
University of Puget Sound, 126, 177
University of Richmond, 12
University of Rochester, 99
University of San Diego, 224
University of San Francisco, 240
University of Scranton, 242
University of South Carolina, 34-35, 184
University of Southern California (USC), 36, 175-176, 181, 242
University of Texas, 35, 118, 188
University of Texas, Austin, 80, 90, 115, 156, 237
University of Texas, San Antonio, 179
University of Vermont, 35
University of Virginia, 12, 34-35, 51, 108, 132, 172, 190
University of Washington, 38, 43
University of Wisconsin, 34-35, 108, 125, 188
unsubsidized Stafford Loans, 245
Ursinus College, 174
U.S. Air Force Academy, 148, 191
U.S. Coast Guard Academy, 148, 191
U.S. Military Academy (West Point), 86, 191
U.S. Naval Academy, 86, 170, 190
U.S. News & World Report rankings, 159
  Baylor University example, 169-170
  categories in, 177-178
  drawbacks of, 169-174
factors in, 171-172
USC (University of Southern California), 36, 175-176, 181, 242
used textbooks, new textbooks versus, 60
UTMA (Uniform Transfer to Minors Act). *See* custodial accounts

V

Vanderbilt University, 132, 172
Vassar College, 10, 115, 191
Vedder, Richard, 179
Villanova University, 125, 151, 242
Virginia Tech University, 172
virtual college visits, 160, 229

visiting colleges
  tips for, 227-229
  virtual college visits, 160, 229
  when to visit, 226-227

W

Wabash College, 145-146
WACAC (Western Association for College Admission Counseling), 202
Wake Forest University, 80, 83
Warren Wilson College, 61
Washington and Lee University, 142, 191
Washington Center for Improving the Quality of Undergraduate Education, 184
Washington University (St. Louis), 12, 96, 117, 181
Wayne State University, 118
wealthy students. *See* rich students
Weaver, Karen, 97
Wellesley College, 11, 115
Wesleyan University, 146, 191
West Point. *See* U.S. Military Academy (West Point)
West Virginia University, 72
Western Association for College Admission Counseling (WACAC), 202
Western Carolina State University, 135
Western Illinois University, 93
Western New England University, 237
Western Undergraduate Exchange, 43
Wheaton College, 167
Whitman College, 172, 228, 232
Whitworth University, 80
Widener University, 242
Willamette University, 177, 228
William Smith College, 181
William Woods University, 232
Williams College, 10, 96, 146, 181, 187, 191
Worcester Polytechnic Institute, 80
Work Colleges Consortium, 61
working colleges, 60-61
writing college essays, 222-225
writing-intensive courses, 185

X–Y–Z

Xavier University, 151, 159

Yale University, 11-12, 64, 66, 121, 141, 146, 175-177, 191, 195, 222
Yeshiva University, 172
YOUniversity
  TV website, 218, 229

Zinch website, 218